D0787439

Guide to U.S. Architecture: 1940–1980

Guide to U.S. Architecture: 1940–1980

by Esther McCoy
and Barbara Goldstein

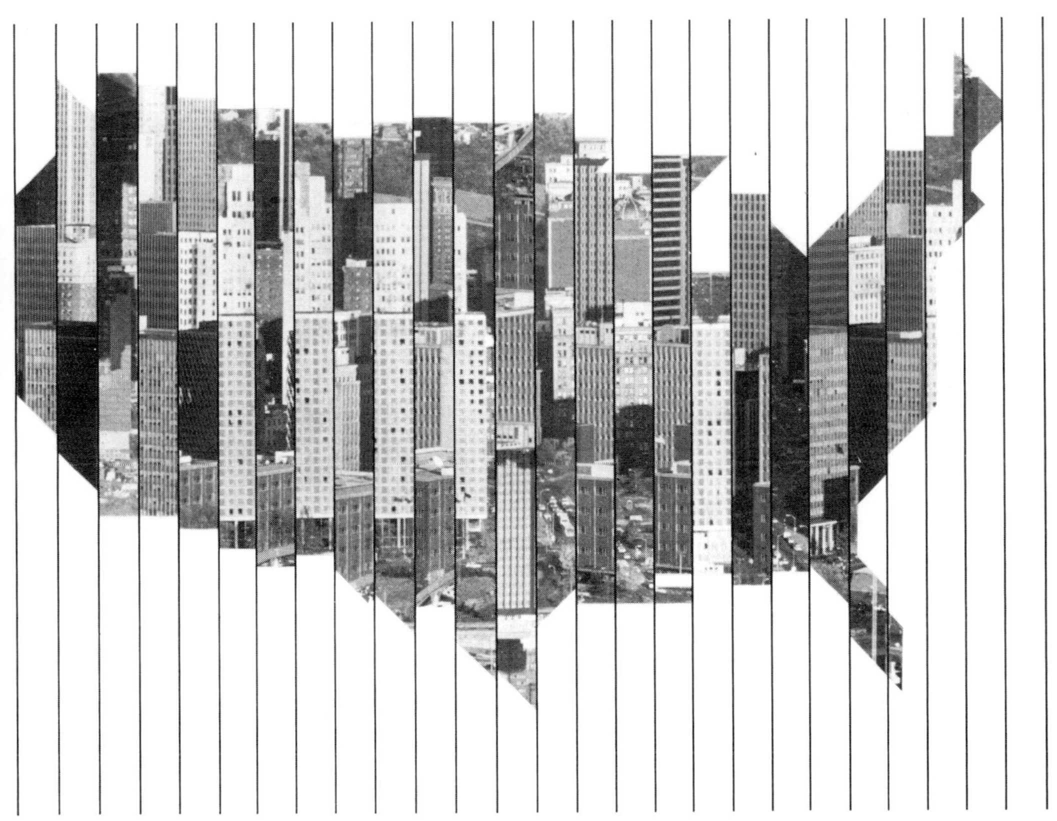

Arts + Architecture Press
Santa Monica, California

Arts + Architecture Press
Santa Monica, California 90401

Printed in the United States of America

Cataloguing in Publication Data

McCoy, Esther
Goldstein, Barbara
Guide to U.S. Architecture 1940–1980.
Bibliography.
Includes indices.
1. Architecture–U.S.–Guide-books.
I. Title.

Library of Congress Catalog Card Number 80-67534
ISBN 0-931228-06-9

Designed by Joe Molloy

Contents

F O R E W O R D

When we first began assembling this guide to contemporary American architecture, we were faced with two enormous questions: why produce such a document in the first place and how to go about doing it?

The first question was easy to answer: no such guidebook currently exists. Although there are travel guides, regional guides, congratulatory guides produced by local architectural societies, guides to historical architecture, at this writing there is no guidebook intended for use in the field by the traveler with a particular interest in contemporary architecture.

This guide does not pretend to be encyclopedic. It is selective, portable and is perhaps most useful because it gives the exact address of listed buildings and shows a picture of almost every one. The reader can judge in advance whether the building is of interest. In the case of major cities, locations are shown on street maps, allowing the traveler to group his site visits efficiently.

The book gives an overview, representing important contemporary buildings throughout the country and provides a bibliography of local guidebooks in the event the traveler wishes to examine the architecture of a city or region in greater depth.

This is a pocket book–a field manual for people in search of those architectural trends which have found realization during the last forty years. Convenient to use and simple to read, it provides the first clues to a more detailed quest.

Deciding which buildings to include in the guide was a very difficult problem. While some cities are virtual museums of contemporary architecture, others have fewer examples of remarkable new buildings. While in the former case we felt obliged to be critically selective, in the latter we had to make subjective decisions about our choices. This led to debates and compromises. A building which was highly acclaimed in 1966 might seem ordinary in 1981, but it may have been seminal–the first to use a particular structural system or to adopt a certain attitude toward its site. The Seagram Building, for example, which spawned many imitations, set a precedent for new forms of urban setbacks. Other buildings have been cannibalized and copied so frequently that the original idea is sullied.

A few other buildings demonstrating new land uses were Roche and Dinkeloo's Ford Foundation Building in New York, which introduced the large, glass-roofed entrance court to a tight urban setting; and Smith, Jones and Contini's Mutual Housing, Los Angeles, the first large scale suburban housing development which fitted the houses to the hillside sites, leaving the valleys as a wild park; and John Lautner's Chemosphere houses in the Hollywood Hills which are supported on a single concrete mast.

Some buildings are included because they signified the turning point in an architect's career: Louis I. Kahn's 1959 Jewish Community Center Bath House, Trenton, NJ; Robert Venturi's 1964 house for his mother (Venturi & Rauch), Philadelphia; and Cesar Pelli's 1976 Pacific Design Center, Los Angeles (Gruen Associates).

Others are here because they marked a change in direction that was important in architectural or planning history: Victor Gruen's 1954 Northland Shopping Center, Detroit; Eero Saarinen's 1962 TWA Terminal at Kennedy Airport; John Portman's 1967 Peachtree Center, Atlanta; Roche and Dinkeloo's 1968 Oakland Museum; and Moore, Lyndon, Turnbull and Whitaker's 1965 Sea Ranch, Gualala, California.

Still others are here because they used old forms in new ways, new places, as Frank Lloyd Wright's anti-urban spiral for Fifth Avenue, New York, in the Guggenheim Museum. Or Bertrand Goldberg's cylindrical apartment towers in Marina City, Chicago. Or the Lakepoint Tower in Chicago (John Heinrich and George Schipporeit) based on Mies's famous free form glass tower projects of the 1920s that were never built.

Others, like Buckminster Fuller, are here because the examples cited are a further refinement and exploration of an idea which carried them through their entire careers.

We have included a type missing from most guides during the heroic period of modern architecture–the regional building. Some areas, particularly California and the South, were always receptive to regional styles, giving them a place with "official" architecture. To the purist of the 1930s wood was synonymous with regional, which automatically excluded architects working in the Bay Area style in northern California until William Wilson Wurster broke the barrier; and in southern California the followers of Greene and Greene had short shrift until Harwell Harris and a few others working in wood were admitted.

But we passed over much of Pop architecture. This, along with craftsmen's houses, has been lovingly observed by David Gebhard and Robert Winter in their guide "Architecture in Los Angeles and Southern California," and Winter's "The California Bungalow." John Margolies continues to collect Pop in all forms throughout the United States; and Charles Jencks brings a reluctant scholarship to the Pop of postmodern. John Pastier's collection of 20,000 old and new postcards from city, town and hamlet across the country is the backbone of a popular history of American urban development. John Chase and John Beach have explored such architectural byways as decorator's houses and set design architecture. We leave all these fields to them.

We have eliminated from the guide a number of important buildings which are difficult to reach and may not be entered if you do. Many good houses have been excluded because they are screened from view by planting or fences, and visitors are not welcome. As guides multiply themselves throughout the country the patience of many owners of famous houses has run out. But often a study of the exterior is reward enough for the visit.

In looking for buildings to include in the guide, we drew on many sources: our own travels, the experience of many advisors, and on publications. Some architects who have reached international stature are represented by a large number of buildings across the country. We felt that if an architect was celebrated enough for his work to extend from Maine to Oregon, it would probably be worth a look.

Architecture is not distributed democratically, the best being heavily weighted to the major cities and to the east and west coasts. But the democratic principle dies hard. Therefore it was with some distress that we noted some of the fifty states were under-represented in our first draft, or had no entries at all. To some extent we have corrected this, and hope for outraged notices of omissions before the second edition.

It was not only a geographic distribution that we looked for but a balanced age distribution as well. Controversy ensued among the editors and their friends as to what was a flash in the pan or a serious first step. (Lou Kahn once said that if an architect's first building was good it was pretty sure to have been borrowed, for as architects are finding their way in their first building it rarely comes off.) Much of the work of the young architects tends to be witty, but nothing falls flatter than the wit of a previous decade. Taken out of context, the bon mot building often has to be explained to the next generation. (Some buildings become unintentionally funny with age.) Thus the buildings for Best Company may fall flat in 1995 if the jokes have to be explained. The situation is somewhat different with the Frank Gehry houses with their exposed lath and chain link fencing: the practice and the materials are comments on the inflation of the economy and the decline of craftsmanship, which may lead the way to other solutions to the same universal problem.

Another consideration was a democratic approach to building types. There were enough friendly advisors around to deplore each type, from brutalist concrete to tight glass skin to exposed steel framing and mechanical systems.

So the principles at work in the selection of buildings for this guide were geographic distribution, inclusion of the work of the young, and no weighting of the guide to a few structural types. This last criterion can be stated negatively: you'll pass it on the way to something else. Or it's in the guide because it's big and it's up.

If we are fortunate, the guide will be what John Ashbery called "a bag into which anything is dumped and ends up belonging there." If our sensibilities have been too hospitable or restrictive the users of the guide will be quick to fault us.

Esther McCoy
Barbara Goldstein

P R E F A C E

Lorsque nous avons commencé à monter ce guide d'architecture américaine, nous nous sommes trouvés devant deux questions énormes: tout d'abord, pourquoi sortir un tel document et comment s'y prendre pour le faire?

Ce fut facile de répondre à la première question: Un tel guide n'a pas existé actuellement. Quoiqu'il y aient des guides de voyage, des guides régionaux, des guides congratulatoires fournis par des sociétés d'architecture locale, et des guides d'architecture historique, il n'existe pas de guide à l'intention du touriste particulièrement intéressé dans l'architecture contemporaine.

Ce guide n'a pas l'intention d'être encyclopédique. Il est sélectif, portatif et est, peut-être, le plus utile, puisqu'il donne l'adresse exacte des édifices enregistrés et montre une photographie de chacun d'eux. Le lecteur peut juger à l'avance si l'edifice est intéressant. Dans le cas de villes les plus grandes, les locations sont indiquées sur des plans, ce qui permet au touriste de grouper efficacement ses visites de site.

Ce livre présente une vue d'ensemble des édifices contemporains importants à travers le pays, et fournit une bibliographie des guides locaux dans le cas où le voyageur veut examiner plus en détail l'architecture d'une ville où d'une région.

C'est un livre de poche, un manuel pour les personnes en quête de ces tendances architecturales qui ont fait jour durant les quarante dernières années. Pratique à l'emploi et simple à lire, il fournit les premiers indices en vue d'une recherche plus complète.

Décider quels édifices faire figurer dans le guide fut un problème difficile! Tandis que certaines villes sont de virtuels musées d'architecture contemporaine, d'autres possèdent peu d'exemples d'édifices nouveaux remarquables. Alors que dans le premier cas, nous nous sommes sentis obligés d'être sévèrement sélectifs, dans le dernier cas, nous avons dû prendre des décisions subjectives quant à notre choix. Ceci entraîna débats et compromis. Un édifice hautement apprécié en 1966 pourrait paraître quelconque en 1981, mais il peut avoir été séminal, en premier lieu d'utiliser un système structural particulier ou bien d'adopter une certaine attitude en raison de son site. Le Seagram Building, par exemple, qui engendra beaucoup d'imitations a établi un précédent pour de nouvelles formes de retours urbains. On a si souvent usurpé et copié les éléments singuliers de certains autres édifices qu'on en a souillé l'idée originale.

Quelques autres édifices illustrant l'utilisation de terrains nouveaux furent: le Ford Foundation Building à New York de Roche et Dinkeloo introduisant au strict cadre urbain les hall d'entrée à grande verrière, et Mutual Housing de Smith, Jones et Contini à Los Angeles, premier développement à grande échelle de résidences suburbaines qui nicha les maisons aux flancs de côteaux, laissant les vallées à l'état de parcs sauvages, ou bien les maisons "Chemosphere" de John Lautner, dans les collines de Hollywood qui ne sont soutenues que par un pilier de béton.

Quelques édifices figurent dans le guide parce qu'ils indiquent un nouveau tournant dans la carrière d'un architecte: les thermes de Jewish Community Center de Louis I. Kahn 1959 à Trenton, New Jersey, la maison de Robert Venturi, 1964 (pour sa mère) Venturi-Rauch, à Philadelphie, le Pacific Design Center de Cèsar Pelli, 1976, à Los Angeles (Gruen Associates).

D'autres y sont indiqués parce qu'ils ont marqué un changement d'orientation important dans l'histoire de l'architecture ou dans l'histoire de l'urbanisme: Northland Centre Commercial, 1954 de Victor Gruen à Detroit, TWA terminal, 1962, à l'aéroport Kennedy de Eero Saarinen, le Peachtree Center de John Portman, 1967 à Atlanta, le musée de Roche et Dinkeloo, 1968 à Oakland, Sea Ranch à Gualala en Californie de Moore, Lyndon, Turnbull et Whitaker, 1965.

D'autres encore y figurent parce qu'ils ont employé des formes anciennes avec des méthodes nouvelles, de nouveaux endroits, telle la spirale anti-urbaine pour Fifth Avenue de Frank Lloyd Wright à New York au musée Guggenheim, ou les tours d'appartement cylindriques de Bertrand Goldberg à Marina City à Chicago, ou bien la tour Lakepoint de John Heinrich et George Schipporeit à Chicago, basée sur les fameux plans de tour de verre sans armature des années 1920, de Mies Van der Rohe qui ne furent jamais exécutés.

D'autres, tel Buckminster Fuller, y sont indiqués parce que les exemples cités représentent davantage un raffinement et une exploration plus poussés d'une idée qui les a transportés à travers leur entière carrière.

Nous y avons inclus un style omis de la plupart des guides pendant la période héroique de l'architecture moderne: l'édifice régional. Quelques régions comme la Californie et le Sud en particulier, ont toujours bien accueilli les styles régionaux leur donnant une place au rang de l'architecture "officielle." Pour le puriste des années 1930, le bois était le synonyme de régional, ce qui excluait automatiquement les architectes travaillant dans le style "Bay Area" au nord de la Californie jusqu'à ce que William Wilson Wurster franchisse les barrières et que, au sud de la Californie, les disciples de Greene et Greene se fassent envoyés au diable jusqu'à ce que Harwell Harris ainsi que quelques autres travaillant avec le bois se fassent acceptés.

Mais nous avons laissé passer beaucoup d'architecture "Pop"; celle-ci, ainsi que les maisons "craftsmen" ont été observées avec soin par David Gebhard et Robert Winter dans leur guide "l'architecture à Los Angeles et dans le sud de la Californie" et dans celui de Winter "le Bungalow de Californie." John Margolies continue à collectionner le "Pop" sous toutes ses formes à travers les Etats Unis et Charles Jencks apporte une érudition réfrènée au "Pop" du post-moderne. La collection de 20.000 cartes postales, anciennes et récentes, de villes, villages et hameaux à travers le pays que possède John Pastier, est le pivot de l'histoire populaire du développement urbain américain. John Chase et John Beach ont exploré quelques à-côtés architecturaux tels que des maisons de décorateurs et l'architecture de plateau du cinema. Nous leur laissons toutes ces spécialités.

Nous avons éliminé du guide une liste d'édifices importants qui sont difficiles d'accès et qu'on ne peut pas visiter même si l'on essaie. Plusieurs maisons intéressantes sont exclues parce qu'elles sont cachées de la vue par des plantations ou des barrières et que les visiteurs n'y sont pas les bienvenus! Comme les guides se multiplient d'eux-mêmes à travers le pays, beaucoup de propriètaires de ces célèbres maisons s'en sont fatigués. Mais bien souvent l'étude de l'extérieur récompense suffisamment pour le déplacement.

Nous avons puisé dans de nombreuses sources, tels que nos propres voyages, l'expérience de nombreux conseillers et des publications pour la recherche des édifices à inclure dans le guide. Quelques architectes qui ont atteint une envergure internationale sont représentés par un grand nombre d'édifices à travers le pays. Nous avons pensé que si un architecte était amplement louangé pour son oeuvre que s'étend du Maine à l'Oregon, cela vaudrait la peine d'être vu.

L'architecture n'est pas distribuée démocratiquement, la meilleure étant lourdement concentrée dans les villes importantes et sur les côtes Est et Ouest. Mais le principe démocratique demeure inébranlable. Toutefois, nous fûmes peinés de noter que quelques uns des cinquante états étaient sous-représentés dans notre première ébauche ou n'avaient pas d'inscription du tout. Nous avons corrigé cela jusqu'à un certain point et espérons des correspondances outragés à ce sujet avant la seconde édition.

Nous n'avons pas seulement recherché une répartition géographique mais une répartition chronologique équilibrée. Il s'en suivit des controverses parmi les éditeurs et leurs amis quant à ce qui fut un feu de paille ou un premier pas sérieux. (Lou Kahn a dit une fois que si le premier édifice d'un architecte était bon, il était presque certain qu'il avait été emprunté, du fait qu'il est rare que des architectes trouvent leur voie dans leur premier édifice.) Une grande partie de l'oeuvre des jeunes architectes tend a être pleine d'esprit mais rien ne tombe plus haut que le bel esprit d'une décade antérieure. Pris hors du sujet, le bon mot édifice doit être expliqué à la prochaine génération. (Quelques édifices deviennent drôles avec l'age sans le vouloir.) Ainsi, les êdifices de Best Company peuvent se retrouver bien bas en 1995 si les plaisanteries doivent être expliquées. La situation est quelque peu différente en ce qui concerne les maisons de Frank Gehry avec leurs lattes à vue et leurs clôtures de chaînes: La pratique et les matériaux dénotent l'inflation de l'économie et le déclin de la connaissance d'un métier superbe ce qui peut ouvrir la voie à d'autres solutions du même problème universel.

Une autre préoccupation a été l'approche démocratique dans le type de construction. Il y avait assez de conseillers bienveillants autour de nous pour déplorer chaque type, du béton brut au peau de verre tendu jusqu'á l'armature de fer et les systémes mécaniques à nu.

Ainsi, les principes en vigueur concernant le choix des édifices de ce guide furent: la répartition géographique, l'inclusion du travail des jeunes et aucun penchant de ce guide pour quelques types structuraux. Ce dernier critère peut-être déclaré négativement: Vous le passerez en route pour quelque chose d'autre, ou bien c'est dans le guide parce que c'est grand et c'est debout.

Si nous avons de la chance, ce guide sera ce que John Ashbery appelait "un sac dans lequel on décharge n'importe quoi et qui finit par y appartenir." Si notre susceptibilité a été trop hospitalière ou bien restrictive, les utilisateurs de ce guide seront rapides à nous blâmer.

Esther McCoy
Barbara Goldstein

前書

現代アメリカ建築の案内書作成にあたり，私共はまず二つの大きな疑問に直面致しました。一つは何故そんなものを作るのかという事。そして今一つは，どうやってそれを作り出すかという事でした。

最初の疑問に対する答は簡単でした。そんな案内書は現在存在しないからです。あるのは旅行ガイド，地域ガイド，各地の建築協会が作っている`御当地´ガイド，歴史的建築ガイド，そして国の建築概要といったもので，現代建築に特別関心を持つ旅行者が利用する目的で作られた案内書は皆無です。

この案内書は百科辞典風のものではありません。読者は好きな個所を選べますし，持ち運びにも便利，且つ記載された建物の正確な住所が殆ど全部写真入りで記されていますので，恐らくは，最も有益な案内書といえます。読者には前以って建物が興味深いものであるかどうかの判断を載けます。大都市の場合は，旅行者に能率的に訪問個所を分類して載く為，各々の場所が地図に示されています。

本書は，万一旅行者が或る都市，亦は或る地方の建築物を詳しく調査したい場合に案内書のリストにもなりますから，アメリカ中の重立った現代建築案内書を代表するものといえます。

これは，過去四十年間の建築の傾向を知りたい人々の為のポケット・ブックなのです。使い易く，読み易く，より詳しく知りたい方々に糸口になってくれます。

どの建物をこの案内書に載せるか決める事は非常な難題でした。幾つかの都市が事実上は現代建築の宝庫である一方，他の都市には秀れた建築の例が少ししかありません。前者の場合私共は厳選を余儀なくされますが，後者では選択する折に主感的な決断を下さざるを得ません。つまり，論争と妥協という事になります。1966年に高い評価を得た建物も，1981年には当り前のものになるかもしれませんが，ある特殊な構造システムを使う時や，配置に対して或る決定を下す時の基礎にはなってきたかもしれません。例えば多くの模倣建築を産み出したシーグラム・ビルディング(Seagram Building)は，都市空間に対する新しい考え方を作り出しました。他の建物でも部分々々を模倣され，それが余りに頻繁になった為，オリジナル・アイディアは傷付けられました。

新しい土地の使い方をしている他の二、三の建物としては，ニュー・ヨークのローチ・アンド・ディッケルー (Roche and Dinkeloo)によるフオード・ファウンデーション・ビルディング (Ford Foundation Building)にみられる狭い都市の条件下での大きなガラス屋根の内庭，亦，ロス・アンジェルスのスミス・ジョーンズ・アンド・コンティーニ (Smith, Jones and Contini) によるミューチュアル・ハウジング (Mutual Housing) にみられるような，谷側は自然のまま残し，山側の土地に家屋を配置させた最初の大規模な効外住宅開発，そしてハリウッド・ヒルズのジョン・ロートナー (John Lautner) によるケモスフェア・ハウス (Chemosphere houses in the Hollywood Hills) にはコンクリートの一本柱が使われています。

1956年，ルイス・カーン (Louis I. Kahn) 設計によるニユー・ジャージー州トレントンのジューウィッシュ・コミュニテイ・センター・バス・ハウス (Jewish Community Center Bath House, Trenton, NJ) や，1964年，ロバート・ヴェンチューリ (Robert Venturi) による彼の母親の為のフィラデルフィアの住宅 (Venturi & Rauch) ，亦，1971年，シーザー・ペリ (Cesar Pelli) によるロス・アンジェルスのパシフイック・デザイン・センター (Pacific Design Center, Los Angeles, Gruen Associates) 等も建築家の経歴の上で転換点となっている意味で上記のものに加えられます。

その他に，建築や都市計画上重要な方向転換を示したものとして，1954年，ヴィクター・グルーエン (Victor Gruen) のノースランド・シヨッピング・センター (Northland Shopping Center, Detroit) ，1962年，イーロー・サーリネン (Eero Saarinen) の TWA ターミナル (TWA Terminal at Kennedy Airport) ，1966年，ジョン・ポートマン (John Portman) のピーチトリー・センター (Peachtree Center, Atlanta)，1968年，ローチ・アンド・デイッケルーのオークランド博物館 (Oakland Museum) ，そして同年，ムーア，リンドン，ターンブル・アンド・ウイッテイカー (Moore, Lyndon, Turnbull and Whitaker) のシー・ランチ (Sea Ranch, Gualala, California) があげられます。

また，フランク・ロイド・ライト (Frank Lloyd Wright) によるニュー・ヨーク，五番街のグーゲンハイム博物館 (Guggenheim Museum) に於る反都市的な螺旋形のように，新しい方法と新しい場所に古い形を使ったものもあります。或いは，シカゴのマリナ・シテイにあるバートランド・ゴールドバーグ (Bertrand Goldberg) の円筒形アパートもありますし，遂に完成をみなかったミース (Mies) の1920年の無形ガラス・タワー・プロジエクトに基いたジョン・ハインリック・アンド・ジョージ・シッポライト (John Heinrich and George Schipporeit) のレイクポイント・タワー (Lakepoint Tower, Chicago) もあります。

その他，バックミンスター・フラー (Buckminster Fuller) のように建築家達が生涯をかけて考えたアイディアを更に練り，探求した例もあります。

私共は，近代建築の英雄時代に殆どの案内書に書きもらされてきた地域の建築をもここに載せています。或る地方，特にカリフォルニア州や，南部諸州では，近代建築を地域性のある建築として認めていました。1930年代の純粋主義者にとって，木造は，ウィリアム・ウィルソン・ワースター (William Wilson Wurster) がその壁を破る迄，北部カリフォルニア州の海岸地方スタイルとして建築家達から敬遠されていましたし，南カリフォルニア州では，ハーウェル・ハリス (Harwell Harris) と他の何人かが，木造建築で認められる迄，グリーン兄弟 (Greene and Greene) 派には暫くの反省の時期がありました。

しかしながら私達は多くのポップ建築（通俗建築）も見て参りました。この事は，手工芸家達の住宅と併せてデイヴィッド・ゲブハード (David Gebhard) とロバート・ウィンター (Robert Winter) の案内書 "Architecture in Los Angeles and Southern California" や，ウィンターの "The California Bungalow" の中によく書かれています。ジョン・マーゴリス (John Margolies) はアメリカ中の全てのポップ建築についてよく書いていますし，チャールス・ジエンクス (Charles Jencks) は近代以降，ポップ建築に疑問を持ちながら奨学金を出しています。国中の都市から町，小村落に至る迄新旧の絵葉書を集めて二万枚からなるジョン・パスティア (John Pastier) のコレクションは，アメリカ都市開発の大衆史の中で主軸になっています。ジョン・チエイス (John Chase) とジョン・ビーチ

(John Beach) はこのような建築上の脇道であるインテリア・デコレーターの設計した住宅や舞台装置的建築を研究しています。私共は，そういうものは彼等にまかせておく事に致します。

私共は，捜しにくく，しかも入場出来ない可能性のある多くの重要な建物はこの案内書から削除致しました。多くの秀れた住宅も木々や柵で見えないように隠されている上，訪問者は歓迎されませんので，この本からは除外されています。国中に案内書がふえるにつれ，多くの有名な家の持ち主の忍耐力も尽きてきています。とはいえ，外観を見るだけでも訪問の価値の充分あるものもありますが。

この案内書には，私共自身の旅行やら，多くのアドバイザーの体験やら，出版物から捜し出された建物が載せられています。国際的レベルに達する何人かの建築家達は，夥しい数の建築をアメリカ中に建てていますし，或る建築家等は，東海岸から西海岸迄その仕事の範囲を広げている程有名ですし，恐らくは一見に価すると私共は思います。

建築は，民主的には分布されていません。大都市の周辺と，東海岸側，西海岸側に秀れた建築が見られます。しかしながら民主々義も根強い上に，第一版では五十州の内の何州かは少ししか載せていませんし，亦全く載せられていない州もあるので，或る程度迄私共はその点を修正してきましたが，第二版が出る迄には皆様の御意向に沿えるように修正し直すつもりです。

私共が求めていますのは，単に地理的な分布でなく，バランスのとれた時代の分布でもあるのです。編集者とその友達々の間で，何が線香花火的に終るか，はたまた本当の第一歩になるかの論議が醸し出されました。（ルイス・カーンは且て，建築家の最初の建物は殆どが誰かの真似をしているので，最初の作品には概ね良いものはない，と言っています。）若い建築家の作品の多くは機知に富んでいますが，十年たてばそれも色褪せます。時代が変ってゆくと，うまい建築と言われていたものでも，次の世代にはしばしば説明が必要になってきます。（建物によっては，時代を経た為に面白くなったものもあります。）従って，今話題になっているベスト・カンパニー (Best Company) の建物も，1995年にはうけなくなるかも知れません。状況は，フランク・ゲーリー (Frank Gehry) の露出させた木舞と金網状の柵を使った住宅設計に至って少々変ってきました。技術と材料はインフレ経済と職人気質の低下を物語り，その事はまた，普遍的なその他の問題の解決策へと繋がっていきます。

もう一つの考えは，建物のタイプに対する民主的なアプローチです。うちっ放しのコンクリートから，鉄骨やメカニックを露出させたガラス張りの建築に至る迄，余り賛成できないアドバイザーもおります。

従って，この案内書に載せる建築を選んだ主旨は，若い人の作品を含めて地理的に分布させ，構造的に秀れたものにだけ重きをおいた案内書にはしてありません。亦，最後に申しあげるこの基準は些か消極的かと思いますが，何処かへ秀れた建築を見に行かれる途中にある建築とか，非常に大きいとか，目立つとかいう理由で載せたものもあります。

この案内書が，ジョン・アッシュベリー (John Ashbery) の言った，〝何でもかんでも投げこまれ，それ故に保存される袋〟のように思って戴ければ幸いです。私共の感覚が余りに寛大すぎたり，或いは厳しすぎれば，読者の皆様からすぐにお叱りを載く事と存じます。

エスター・マッコイ (Esther McCoy)
バーバラ・ゴールドスタイン (Barbara Goldstein)

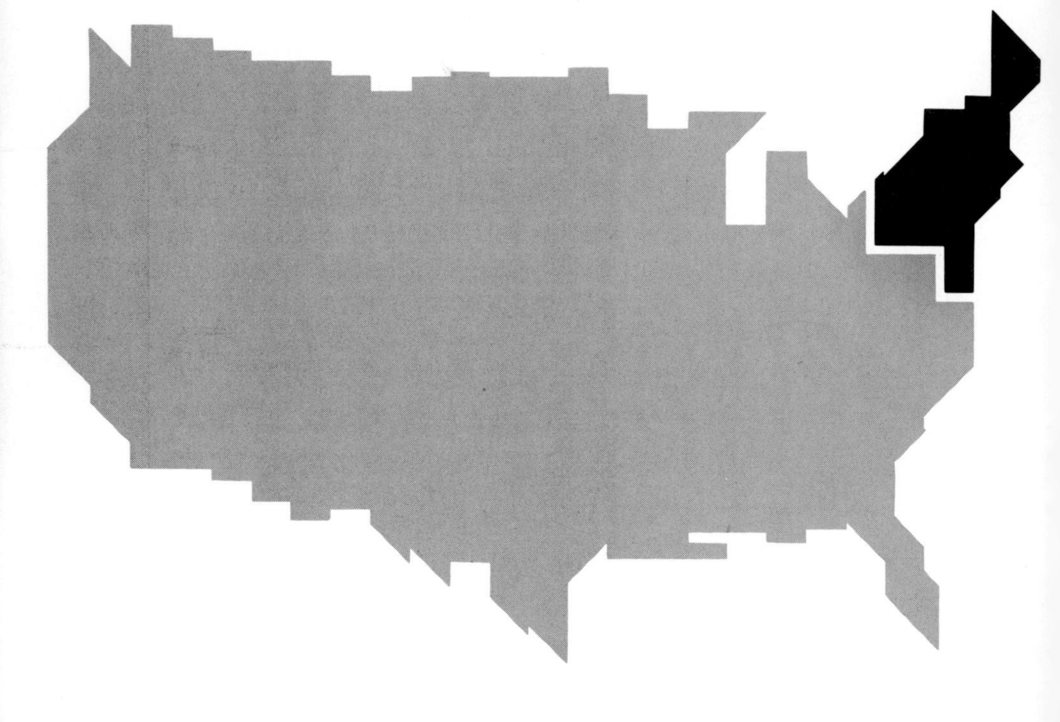

N O R T H E A S T

Maine

Visual Arts Center
Brunswick ME
Bowdoin College
1976
Edward Larrabee Barnes Assoc.

Castine Yacht Club
Castine ME
Water Street
1963
David E. Austin

Haystack Mountain School of Arts and Crafts
Deer Isle ME
Deer Isle
1962
Edward Larrabee Barnes Assoc.

Houlton Regional Hospital
Houlton ME
20 Hartford Street
1976
Payette Associates

New Hampshire

Residence Hall
Durham NH
University of New Hampshire
1974
Ulrich Franzen & Associates

Library

Exeter NH

Phillips Exeter Academy

1972

Louis I. Kahn

Kahn Collection, U of PA

The Village at Loon Mtn.

Lincoln NH

3 miles east of Lincoln

1974–Present

Huygens & Tappe

Steve Rosenthal

Vermont

Dickenson Science Building

Bennington VT

Bennington College

1970

Robertson Ward

George Cserna

Cathedral of the Immaculate Conception

Burlington VT

20 Pine Street

1976

Edward L. Barnes; Colin Lindburg

Nick Wheeler

Massachusetts

Fine Arts Center

Amherst MA

University of Massachusetts

1974

Kevin Roche John Dinkeloo & Associates

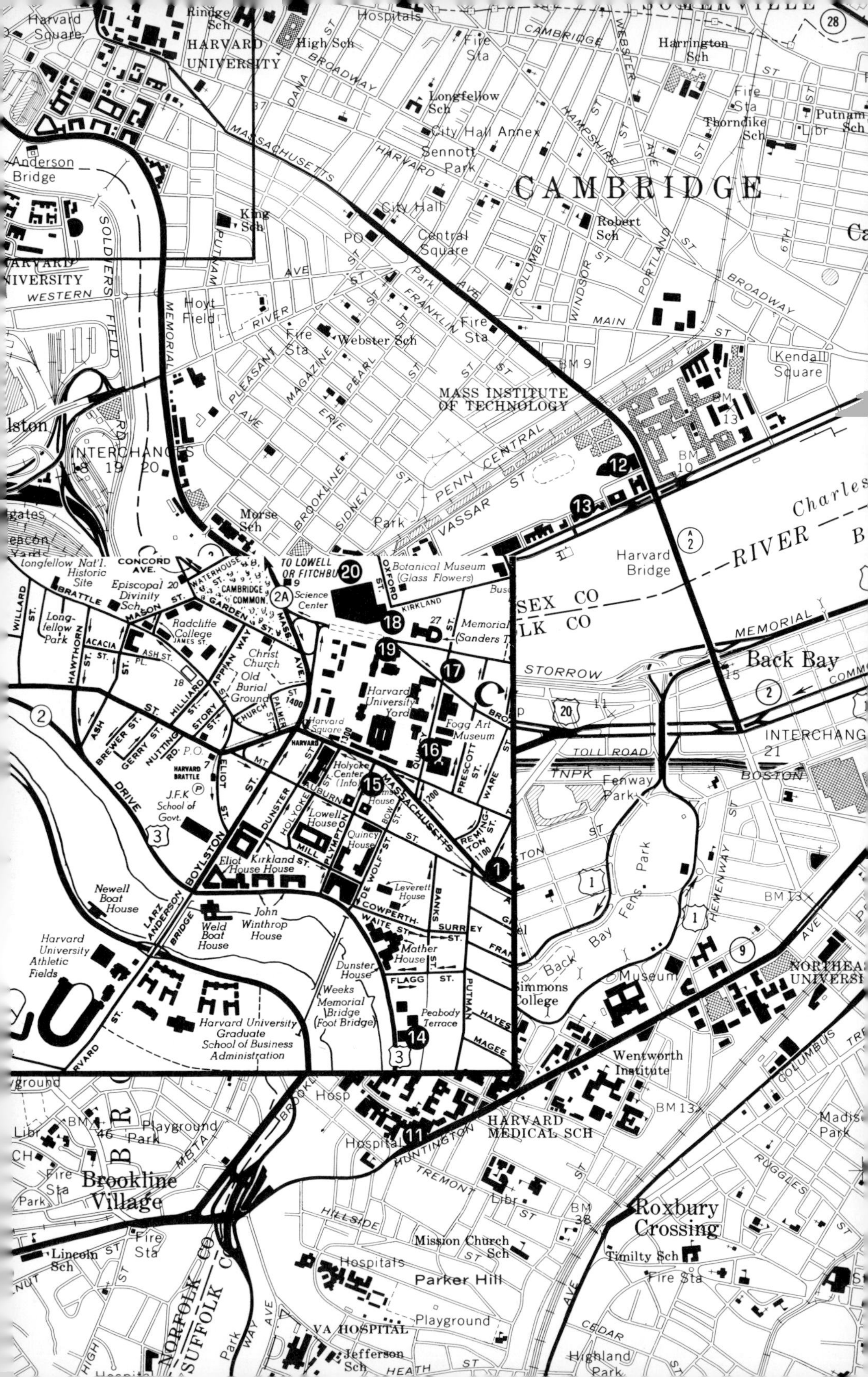

CAMBRIDGE
Harvard Square
HARVARD UNIVERSITY
MASS INSTITUTE OF TECHNOLOGY
Kendall Square
Central Square
City Hall
Charles RIVER
Harvard Bridge
Back Bay
Fenway Park
Back Bay Fens Park
Simmons College
Museum
NORTHEASTERN UNIVERSITY
Wentworth Institute
HARVARD MEDICAL SCH
Roxbury Crossing
Brookline Village
Parker Hill
VA HOSPITAL
Mission Church Sch
NORFOLK CO
SUFFOLK CO
Longfellow Nat'l. Historic Site
Episcopal Divinity Sch
CAMBRIDGE COMMON
Radcliffe College
Christ Church
Old Burial Ground
Science Center
Botanical Museum (Glass Flowers)
Memorial Hall (Sanders Theatre)
Harvard University Yard
Fogg Art Museum
Holyoke Center (Info)
J.F.K. School of Govt.
Eliot House
Kirkland House
Lowell House
Quincy House
Leverett House
Mather House
Dunster House
Peabody Terrace
Weeks Memorial Bridge (Foot Bridge)
Weld Boat House
John Winthrop House
Newell Boat House
Harvard University Athletic Fields
Harvard University Graduate School of Business Administration
TO LOWELL OR FITCHBURG
INTERCHANGES 18 19 20
INTERCHANGE 21

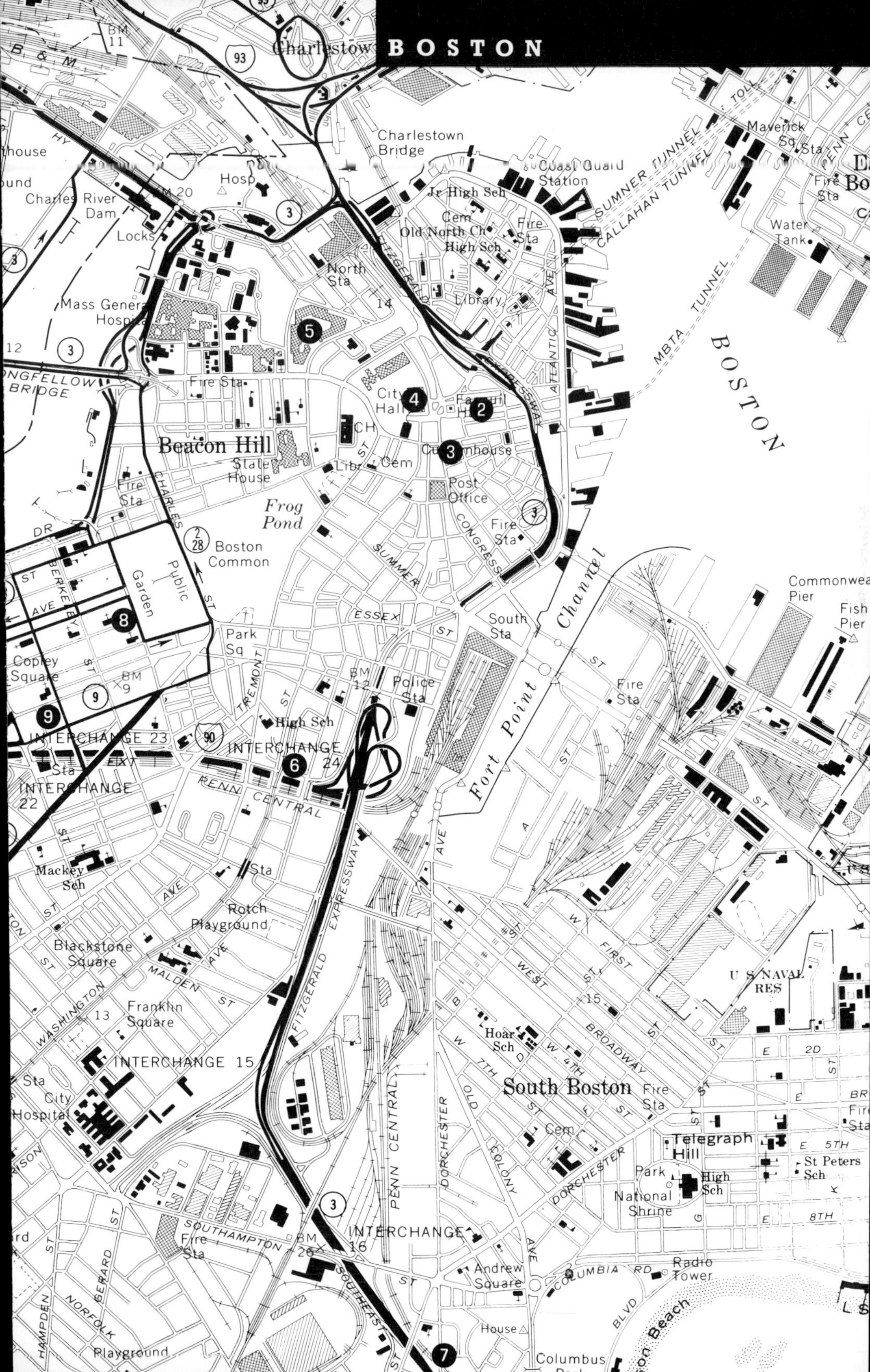

Charlestown
Charlestown Bridge
Coast Guard Station
Jr High Sch
Old North Ch
High Sch
Fire Sta
Library
SUMNER TUNNEL
CALLAHAN TUNNEL
MBTA TUNNEL
Maverick Sq Sta
Water Tank
BOSTON
Charles River Dam
Locks
Hosp
Mass General Hospital
North Sta
LONGFELLOW BRIDGE
Fire Sta
City Hall
Faneuil Hall
Beacon Hill
State House
Customhouse
Post Office
Frog Pond
Boston Common
Public Garden
CHARLES ST
CONGRESS
SUMMER
ESSEX ST
Park Sq
South Sta
Fort Point Channel
Commonwealth Pier
Fish Pier
Copley Square
INTERCHANGE 23
INTERCHANGE 24
INTERCHANGE 22
PENN CENTRAL
Police Sta
High Sch
TREMONT
Mackey Sch
Rotch Playground
Blackstone Square
Franklin Square
MALDEN ST
WASHINGTON
INTERCHANGE 15
City Hospital
FITZGERALD EXPRESSWAY
WEST
FIRST
BROADWAY
U S NAVAL RES
Hoar Sch
South Boston
Telegraph Hill
Park
National Shrine
High Sch
St Peters Sch
DORCHESTER AVE
OLD COLONY
SOUTHAMPTON ST
INTERCHANGE 16
SOUTHEAST
Andrew Square
COLUMBIA RD
Radio Tower
BLVD
House
Columbus Park
Playground
HAMPDEN
NORFOLK
GERARD
1
2
3
4
5
6
7
8
9

Hall Mercer Children's Ctr.

Belmont MA

McClean Hospital

1973

Perry Dean Stahl & Rogers

Phokion Karas

Baker House

Cambridge MA 13

MIT Campus

1947

Alvar Aalto

Gund Hall

Cambridge MA 17

Harvard University

1969

John Andrews

New England Merchants National Bank 3

Boston MA

28 State Street

1971

Edward L. Barnes; Emory Roth

Office Building

Cambridge MA 1

1050 Massachusetts Avenue

1978

Cambridge Seven Associates

Canaday Hall Dormitory

Cambridge MA 19

Harvard University

1974

Ezra D. Ehrenkrantz

Knoll Int'l Showroom/Offices

Boston MA 8

Newbury and Arlington Streets

1978

Gwathmey Siegel & Associates

Steve Rosenthal

Boston Public Library Add'n

Boston MA 10

Copley Square

1973

Johnson/Burgee;

Architects Design Group

Nathaniel Lieberman

City Hall

Boston MA 4

1 City Hall Square

1967

Kallman McKinnell & Knowles

Ezra Stoller©Esto

Carpenter Center

for the Visual Arts 16

Cambridge MA

Harvard University

1961

Le Corbusier

Julius Shulman

John Hancock Tower

Boston MA 9

Clarendon and St. James Street

1976

I. M. Pei & Partners

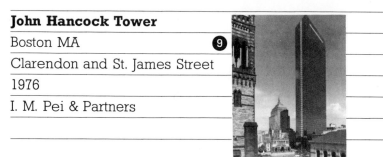

John F. Kennedy Library

Dorchester MA 7

Univ. of Mass. Harbor Campus

1979

I. M. Pei & Partners

Boston State Service Center

Boston MA 5

New Chardon Street

1973

Paul Rudolph; Shepley Bulfinch Richardson & Abbott; Desmond & Lord; M. A. Dyer; Pederson & Tilney

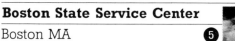

Chapel

Cambridge MA 12

MIT Campus

1954

Eero Saarinen & Associates

Undergraduate Science Ctr.

Cambridge MA 18

Harvard University

1973

Sert Jackson & Associates

Holyoke Center
Cambridge MA 10
1350 Massachusetts Avenue
1966
Sert Jackson & Associates

David Hirsch

Frances Peabody Terrace
Cambridge MA 14
900 Memorial Drive
1966
Sert Jackson & Gourley

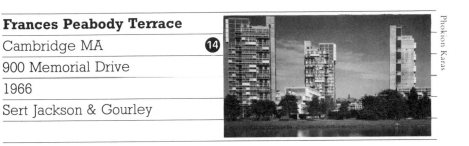

Phokion Karas

Francis A. Countway
Library of Medicine 11
Boston MA
10 Shattuck Street
1965
Hugh Stubbins & Associates

Louis Reens

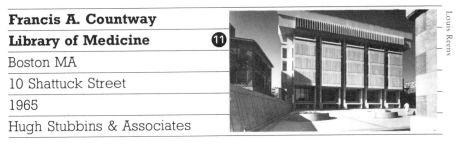

Josiah Quincy
Community School 6
Boston MA
Marginal & Washington Streets
1976
The Architects Collaborative

Steve Rosenthal

Graduate Center
Cambridge MA 20
Harvard University
1949
The Architects Collaborative

Fred Stone

Quincy Market

Boston MA 2

Commercial & Clinton Streets

1975

Benjamin Thompson

Arts & Humanities Building

Dartmouth MA

Southeastern Massachusetts Univ.

1966

Paul Rudolph; Desmond & Lord

Science Center

Wellesley MA

Wellesley College

1979

Perry Dean Stahl & Rogers

Jewett Art Center

Wellesley MA

Wellesley College

1958

Paul Rudolph; Anderson, Beckwith & Haible

Goddard Memorial Library

Worcester MA

Clark University

1970

Johansen & Bhavnani

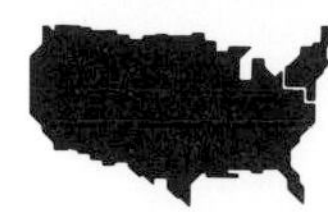

Vorcester County Nat'l Bank

Vorcester MA

46 Main Street

974

Kevin Roche John Dinkeloo

: Associates

Connecticut

Iouse VI

Cornwall CT

Great Hollow Road

976

Peter Eisenman

Richard Frank

Brant House

Greenwich CT

aconic Road

973

Venturi Rauch & Scott Brown

Cervin Robinson

Aetna Life & Casualty

Computer Center

Hartford CT

51 Farmington Avenue

972

evin Roche John Dinkeloo

: Associates

Creative Arts Center

Middleton CT

High and Washington Streets

973

Kevin Roche John Dinkeloo

: Associates

Milford Jai Alai Fronton

Milford CT

311 Old Gate Lane

1979

Herbert S. Newman Associates

Becton Center for Eng'g & Applied Science

New Haven CT

Yale University

1970

Marcel Breuer & Hamilton Smith

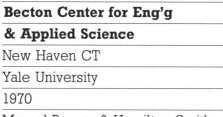

Fire Headquarters

New Haven CT

Grand Avenue at Olive Street

1961

Earl P. Carlin; Peter Millard, Design Associate

Kline Science Center

New Haven CT

Yale University

1965

Philip Johnson & Richard Foster

Yale Art Gallery

New Haven CT

Yale University

1953

Louis I. Kahn

Center for American Arts
New Haven CT
Yale University Art Gallery
1976
Herbert S. Newman Associates

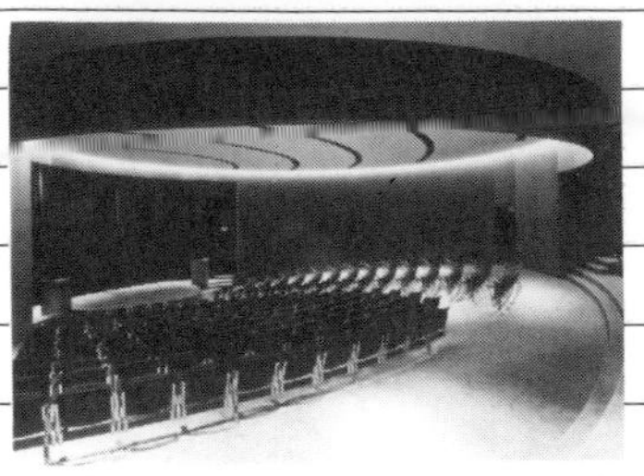

Norman McGrath

Richard C. Lee High School
New Haven CT
100 Church Street South
1967
Kevin Roche John Dinkeloo
& Associates

Knights of Columbus Hdqtrs.
New Haven CT
One Columbus Plaza
1969
Kevin Roche John Dinkeloo
& Associates

Veterans Memorial Coliseum
New Haven CT
275 South Orange Street
1972
Kevin Roche John Dinkeloo
& Associates

Crawford Manor
New Haven CT
90 Park Street
1966
Paul Rudolph

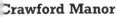

Art & Architecture Building
New Haven CT
Yale University
1964
Paul Rudolph

David S. Ingalls Skating Rink
New Haven CT
Yale University
1958
Eero Saarinen & Associates

Stiles & Morse Colleges
New Haven CT
Yale University
1962
Eero Saarinen & Associates

Computer Center
New Haven CT
Yale University
1961
Skidmore Owings & Merrill

Beinecke Library
New Haven CT
Yale University
1963
Skidmore Owings & Merrill

Dixwell Fire Station

New Haven CT

Goffe and Sperry Streets

1974

Venturi Rauch & Scott Brown

Steven Izenour

Schlumberger-Doll Research Lab

Ridgefield CT

Old Quarry Road

1980

Howard Barnstone

Heritage Village

Southbury CT

Interstate Highway 84

1978

Callister Payne & Bischoff

Richardson-Vicks Hdqtrs.

Wilton CT

10 Westport Road

1974

Kevin Roche John Dinkeloo & Associates

New York

Rockefeller Empire State Plaza

Albany NY

State Street

1978

Harrison & Abramovitz

New York State Bar Center
Albany NY
Elk and Eagle Streets
1972
James Stewart Polshek & Partners

Municipal Fire Hdqtrs. Bldg.
Corning NY
Corning Blvd. & Centerway Bridge
1976
Gunnar Birkerts & Associates

Corning Museum of Glass
Corning NY
Centerway and Pulteney
1980
Gunnar Birkerts & Associates

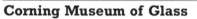

Agronomy Building for Biological Sciences
Ithaca NY
Cornell University
1966
Ulrich Franzen & Associates

Boyce Thompson Institute for Plant Research
Ithaca NY
Cornell University
1978
Ulrich Franzen & Associates

Herbert F. Johnson Museum of Art

Ithaca NY

Cornell University

1973

I. M. Pei & Partners

Hamilton/Cornell Univ.

Olympic Center

Lake Placid NY

Main Street

1980

Hellmuth Obata & Kassabaum

Bill Remington

The Juilliard School

New York NY 20

Lincoln Center Plaza

1969

Pietro Belluschi; E. Catalano & H. Westermann

Ezra Stoller ©Esto

Whitney Museum of Modern Art 24

New York NY

945 Madison Avenue

1966

Marcel Breuer & Hamilton Smith

Ezra Stoller ©Esto

Jehovah's Witness Dormitory and Classroom Building 5

New York NY (Brooklyn)

Pineapple & Columbus Heights

1969

Ulrich Franzen & Associates

George Cserna

NEW JERSEY
NEW YORK
HUDSON CO
NEW YORK CO
RIVER
HUDSON
Castle Point
Castle Stevens
Harsimus Cove
Morris Canal Basin
LEHIGH VALLEY
City Hall
Sch No 1
Sch No 16
WARREN
HOLLAND TOLL TUNNEL
FERRY
NEW YORK CITY BOUNDARY
Fire Boat Sta
Port Authority
Hughes High Sch
PS 70
PS 11
W 18TH ST
W 14TH ST
E 18TH
E 10TH
St Francis Xavier College
Hebrew Center
Armory
Union Sq Park
St Vincents Hospital
Greenwich Village
Washington Sq Park
NEW YORK UNIVERSITY
UNIVERSITY PLACE
W 3D ST
BLEECKER
W HOUSTON
Hudson Park
CHRISTOPHER
PERRY ST
AVENUE OF THE AMERICAS
ELEVATED
SPRING
Tollgate
CANAL ST
LAIGHT ST
HUDSON
WASHINGTON
WEST SIDE
GREENWICH
WEST
BROADWAY
MERCER ST
LAFAYETTE
CHURCH
Welfare Dept
Criminal Court
US Court
City Hall
DEY ST
Police Sta
Trinity Ch
WALL
NASSAU
Beekman Hosp
Bowling Green
Custom House
Battery Park
Castle Clinton Nat Mon
Light
MANHATTAN

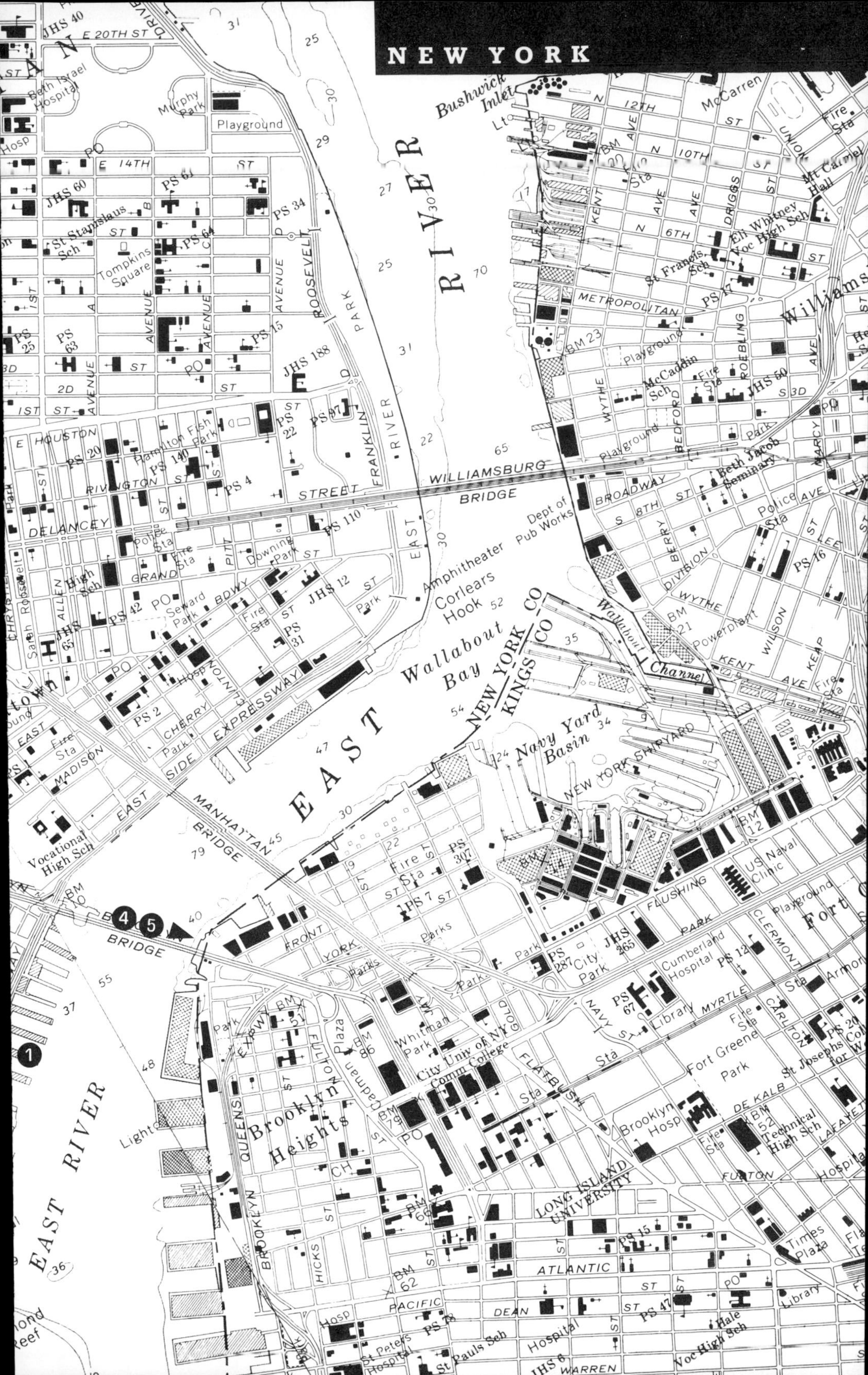
EAST RIVER
Wallabout Bay
Corlears Hook
Bushwick Inlet
Navy Yard Basin
NEW YORK SHIPYARD
Wallabout Channel
WILLIAMSBURG BRIDGE
MANHATTAN BRIDGE
BROOKLYN BRIDGE
NEW YORK CO
KINGS CO
FRANKLIN D ROOSEVELT
EAST RIVER PARK
EAST SIDE EXPRESSWAY
Tompkins Square
Murphy Park
Playground
Beth Israel Hospital
Hamilton Fish Park
Seward Park
Downing Park
Amphitheater
Dept of Pub Works
Vocational High Sch
E 20TH ST
E 14TH ST
E HOUSTON
RIVINGTON
DELANCEY
GRAND
MADISON
CHERRY
STREET
BROADWAY
METROPOLITAN
KENT
WYTHE
BEDFORD
DRIGGS
ROEBLING
DIVISION
BERRY
WILSON
KEAP
MARCY
LEE
FLUSHING
PARK
MYRTLE
CLERMONT
CARLTON
DE KALB
FULTON
ATLANTIC
PACIFIC
DEAN
WARREN
HICKS
QUEENS
FRONT
YORK
JAY
GOLD
NAVY
FLATBUSH
Cadman Plaza
Whitman Park
City Univ of NY
Comm College
Brooklyn Heights
LONG ISLAND UNIVERSITY
Fort Greene Park
Brooklyn Hosp
Cumberland Hospital
Technical High Sch
US Naval Clinic
McCarren
Eli Whitney Voc High Sch
Mt Carmel Hall
St Francis Sch
McCaddin Sch
Beth Jacob Seminary
Powerplant
Times Plaza
St Peters Hospital
St Pauls Sch
Voc High Sch
Williamsburg

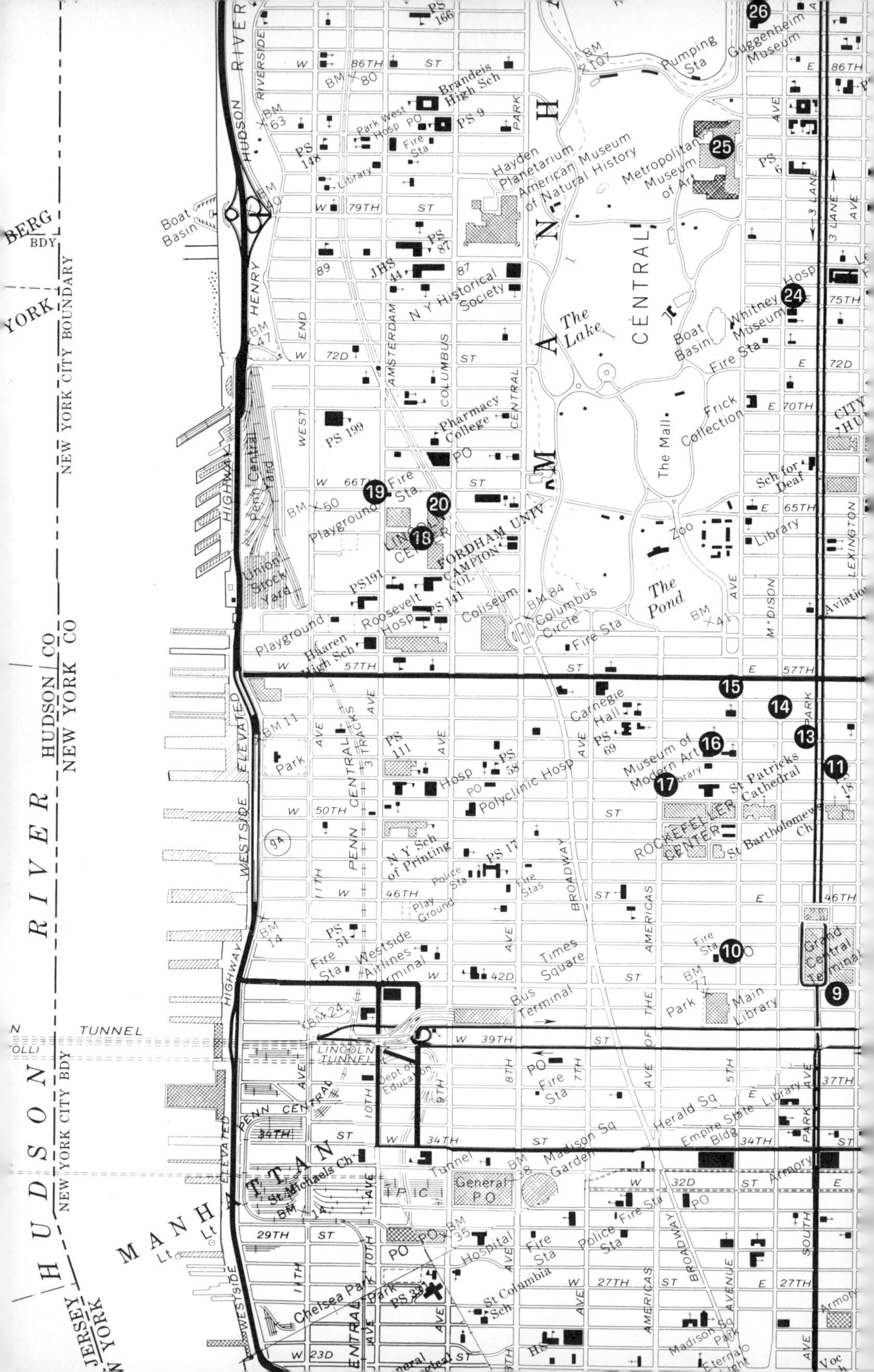
HUDSON RIVER
NEW YORK CITY BOUNDARY
HUDSON CO
NEW YORK CO
NEW YORK CITY BDY
JERSEY
NEW YORK
MANHATTAN
CENTRAL PARK
Boat Basin
Henry Hudson Highway
Westside Elevated Highway
Penn Central Yard
Union Stock Yard
Lincoln Tunnel
Riverside
West End
Amsterdam
Columbus
Central Park
Broadway
Ave of the Americas
5th Avenue
Madison Ave
Park Ave
Lexington
W 86th St
W 79th St
W 72d St
W 66th St
W 57th St
W 50th St
W 46th St
W 42d St
W 39th St
W 34th St
W 32d St
29th St
W 27th St
W 23d St
E 86th
E 75th
E 72d
E 70th
E 65th
E 57th
E 46th
E 37th
E 34th
E 27th
Brandeis High Sch
Park West Hosp PO
Fire Sta
PS 9
PS 148
PS 166
Library
Hayden Planetarium
American Museum of Natural History
Metropolitan Museum of Art
Guggenheim Museum
Pumping Sta
NY Historical Society
JHS 44
PS 87
The Lake
Whitney Museum
Hosp
Boat Basin
Fire Sta
Frick Collection
The Mall
PS 199
Pharmacy College
PO
Sch for Deaf
Playground
Lincoln Center
Fordham Univ Campion Col
Zoo
Library
PS 191
Roosevelt Hosp
PS 141
Coliseum
Columbus Circle
The Pond
Haaren High Sch
Fire Sta
Carnegie Hall
PS 69
Museum of Modern Art
Library
St Patricks Cathedral
Rockefeller Center
St Bartholomews Ch
PS 111
Hosp
PS 58
Polyclinic Hosp
NY Sch of Printing
PS 17
Police Sta
Play Ground
Fire Stas
PS 51
Fire Sta
Westside Airlines Terminal
Times Square
Park
Main Library
Grand Central Terminal
Bus Terminal
Dept of Education
PO
Fire Sta
Herald Sq
Empire State Bldg
Library
Madison Sq Garden
General PO
St Michaels Ch
Tunnel
Armory
Hospital
PO
Police Sta
Fire Sta
Chelsea Park
PS 33
St Columbia Sch
Madison Sq Park
Eternal Light
City Hu
Aviation
Voc

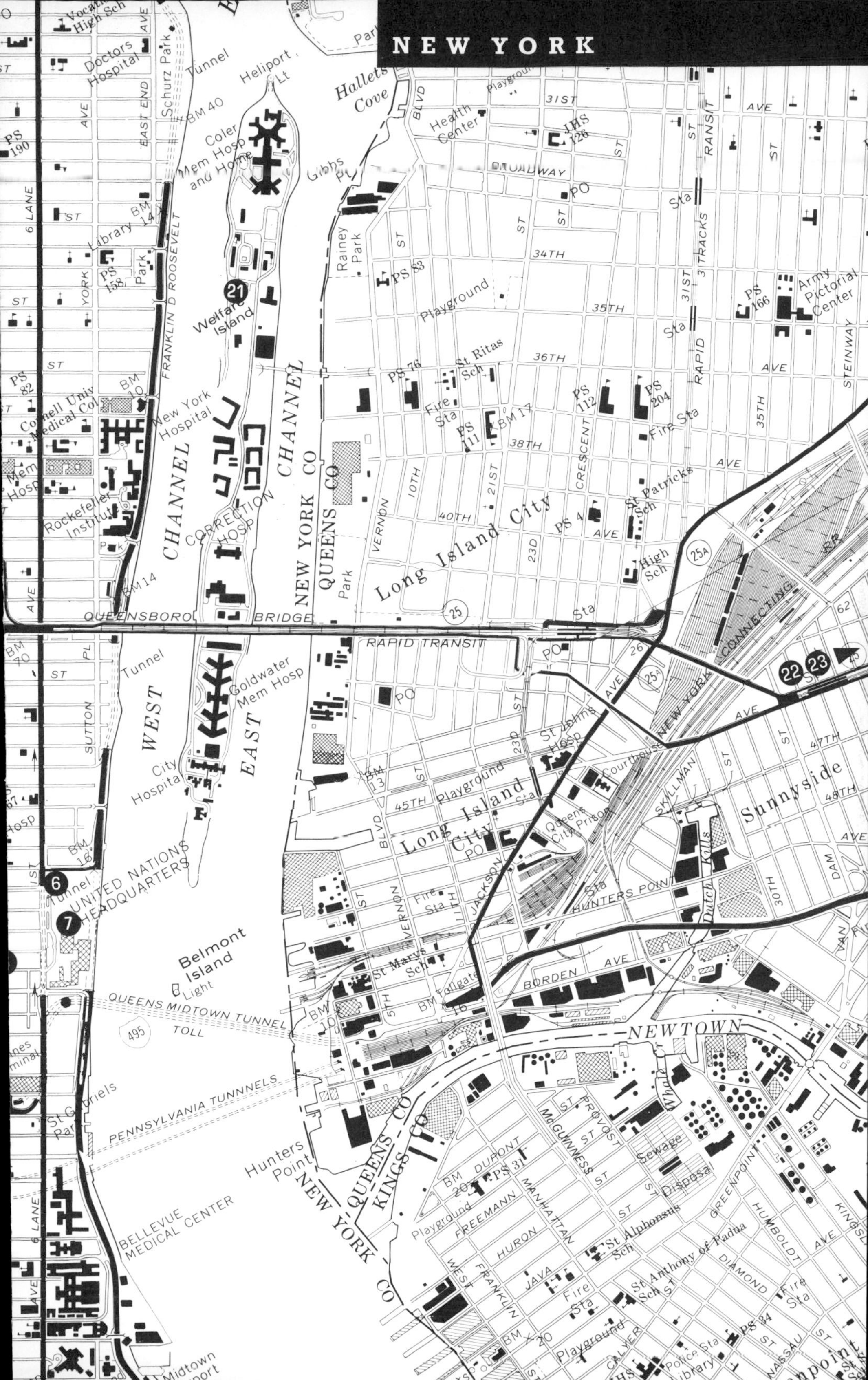
Hallets Cove
Heliport Lt
Doctors Hospital
Schurz Park
Tunnel
Coler Mem Hosp and Home
Gibbs Pt
Rainey Park
PS 83
Playground
Library
PS 158
Welfare Island
21
FRANKLIN D ROOSEVELT
Cornell Univ Medical Col
New York Hospital
Rockefeller Institute
CHANNEL
CORRECTION HOSP
NEW YORK CO
QUEENS CO
St Ritas Sch
PS 76
Fire Sta
PS 111
PS 112
PS 204
Fire Sta
St Patricks Sch
PS 4
High Sch
Long Island City
QUEENSBORO BRIDGE
RAPID TRANSIT
PS 166
Army Pictorial Center
STEINWAY
CRESCENT
VERNON
Goldwater Mem Hosp
WEST
EAST
City Hospital
SUTTON PL
YORK AVE
PS 190
PS 82
CONNECTING RR
NEW YORK
22
23
St Johns Hosp
Courthouse
Queens City Prison
Long Island City
Sunnyside
SKILLMAN
Dutch Kills
HUNTERS POINT
6
7
UNITED NATIONS HEADQUARTERS
Belmont Island Light
QUEENS MIDTOWN TUNNEL TOLL
495
St Marys Sch
BORDEN AVE
NEWTOWN
PENNSYLVANIA TUNNELS
St Gabriels Park
Hunters Point
BELLEVUE MEDICAL CENTER
QUEENS CO
KINGS CO
NEW YORK CO
McGUINNESS
PROVOST
Sewage Disposal
PS 31
DUPONT
FREEMANN
MANHATTAN
HURON
JAVA
St Alphonsus Sch
St Anthony of Padua Sch
GREENPOINT
HUMBOLDT
DIAMOND
Fire Sta
PS 84
Police Sta
Library
CALYER
NASSAU
Playground
Midtown Skyport
Whale Cr

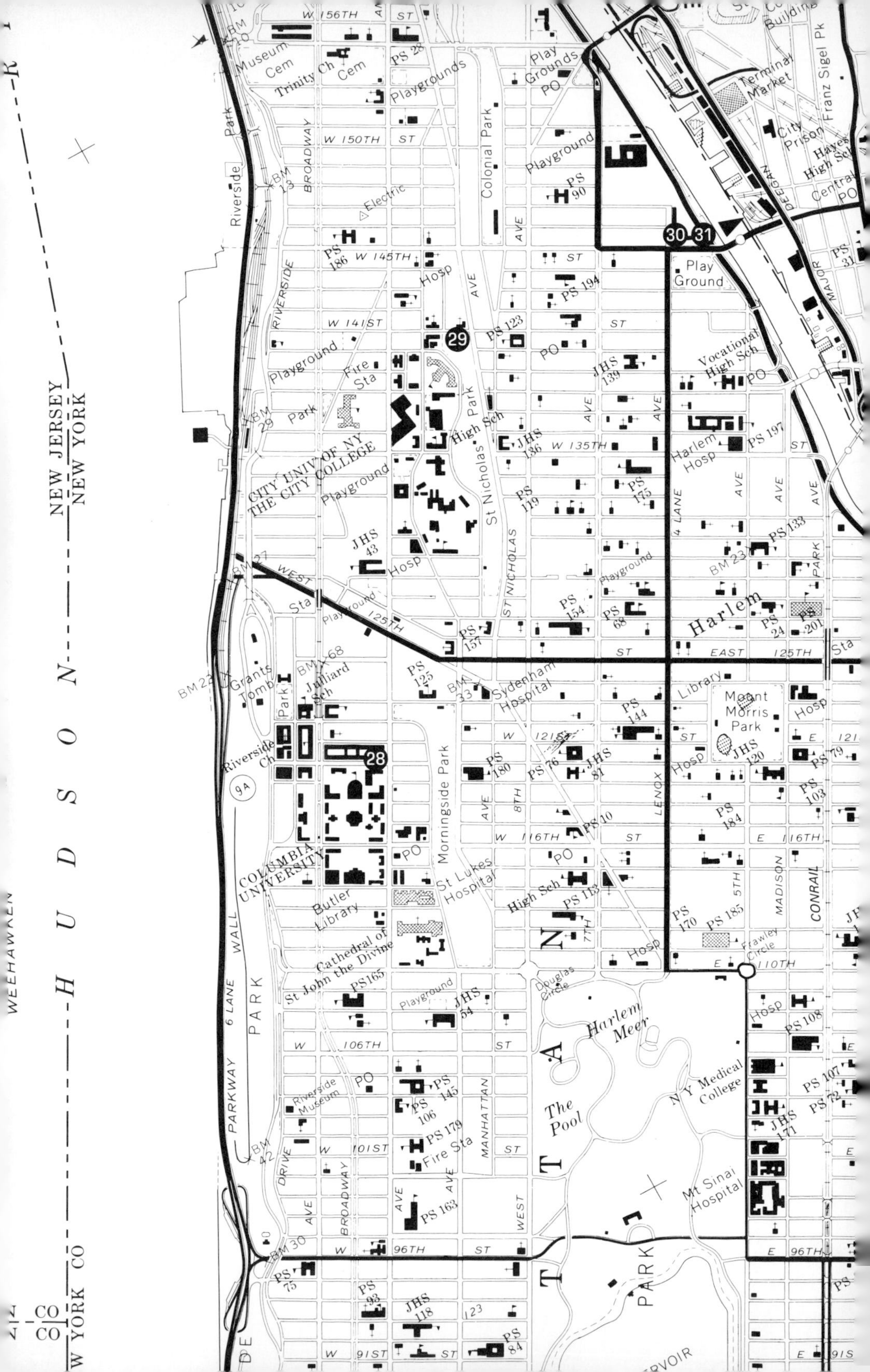

NEW JERSEY
NEW YORK
HUDSON
WEEHAWKEN
NEW YORK CO
W 156TH ST
Museum
Cem
Trinity Ch
Cem
PS 28
Playgrounds
Play Grounds
PO
Colonial Park
Playground
PS 90
W 150TH ST
BROADWAY
Riverside Park
Electric
Terminal Market
Franz Sigel Pk
City Prison
Hayes High Sch
Central PO
DEEGAN
MAJOR
PS 31
30
31
PS 186
W 145TH ST
Hosp
AVE
Play Ground
PS 194
RIVERSIDE
W 141ST
29
PS 123
ST
PO
Playground
Fire Sta
Park
JHS 139
Vocational High Sch
PO
St Nicholas Park
High Sch
JHS 136
W 135TH ST
Harlem Hosp
PS 197
CITY UNIV OF NY THE CITY COLLEGE
Playground
PS 119
PS 175
4 LANE
JHS 43
Hosp
ST NICHOLAS
PS 133
BM 23
PARK
WEST 125TH
Sta
Playground
PS 154
PS 68
Harlem
PS 24
PS 201
PS 157
ST
EAST 125TH
Sta
Grants Tomb
Park
Julliard Sch
PS 125
Sydenham Hospital
Library
Mount Morris Park
Hosp
Riverside Ch
28
9A
W 121ST
PS 144
PS 180
PS 76
JHS 81
JHS 120
PS 79
Morningside Park
8TH
LENOX
PS 103
PS 184
COLUMBIA UNIVERSITY
PO
W 116TH ST
PS 10
E 116TH
PO
St Lukes Hospital
Butler Library
High Sch
PS 113
7TH
5TH
MADISON
CONRAIL
PS 170
PS 185
Cathedral of St John the Divine
Frawley Circle
Hosp
E 110TH
PS 165
Douglas Circle
Playground
JHS 54
Harlem Meer
Hosp
PS 108
PARKWAY 6 LANE WALL
PARK
W 106TH ST
Riverside Museum
PO
PS 145
PS 106
MANHATTAN
The Pool
N Y Medical College
PS 107
PS 72
JHS 171
W 101ST
PS 179
Fire Sta
ST
DRIVE
AVE
BROADWAY
PS 163
WEST
Mt Sinai Hospital
BM 30
W 96TH ST
E 96TH
PS 75
PS 93
JHS 118
123
PS 84
PARK
W 91ST ST
E 91S

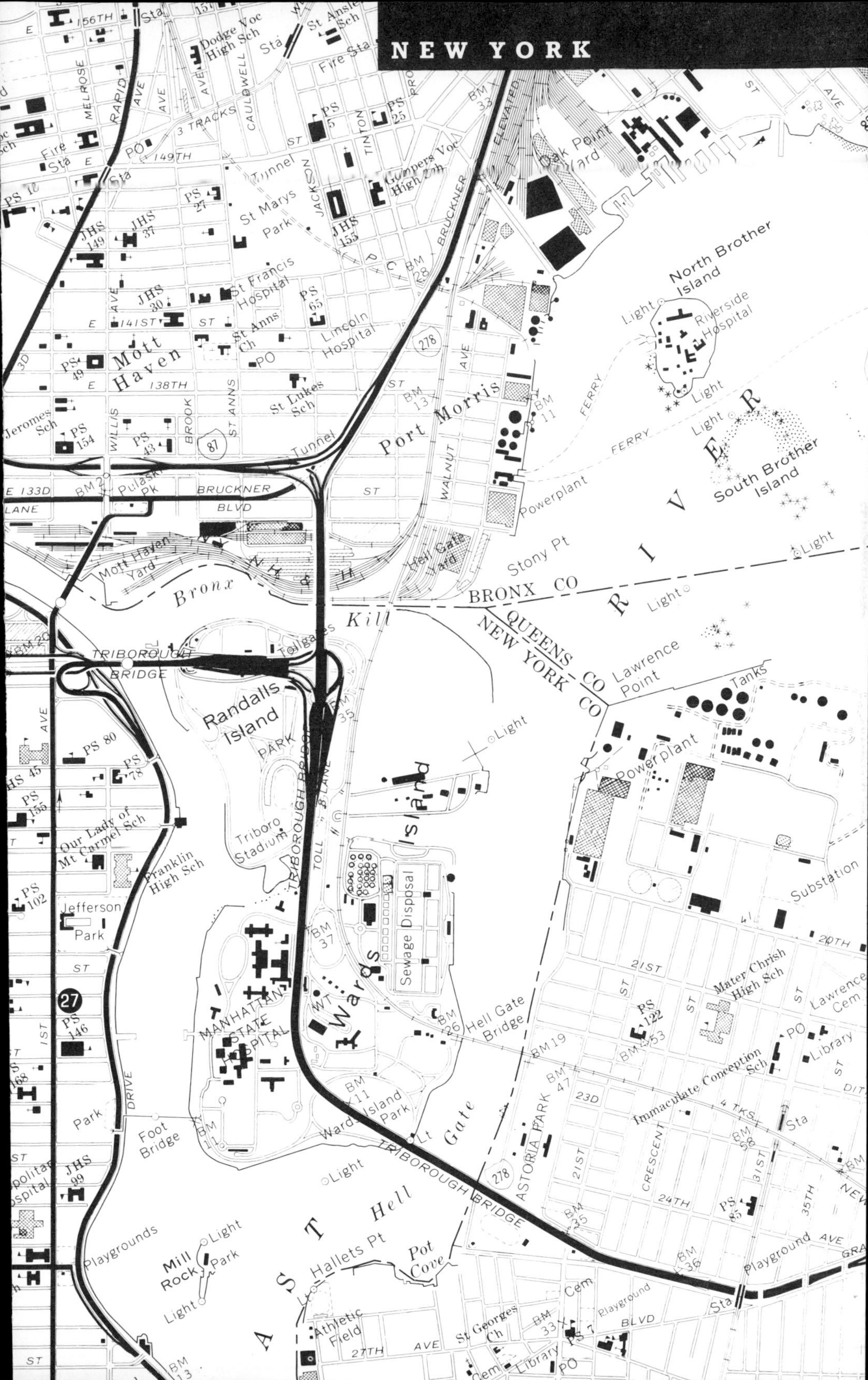
Mott Haven
Port Morris
North Brother Island
Riverside Hospital
South Brother Island
Oak Point Yard
Mott Haven Yard
Hell Gate Yard
Bronx Kill
BRONX CO
QUEENS CO
NEW YORK CO
Stony Pt
Lawrence Point
Tanks
Powerplant
Substation
Randalls Island
PARK
Triboro Stadium
TRIBOROUGH BRIDGE
TOLL LANE
Tollgates
Wards Island
Sewage Disposal
Wards Island Park
MANHATTAN STATE HOSPITAL
Hell Gate Bridge
Hell Gate
Lt
Light
Mill Rock Park
Hallets Pt
Pot Cove
Athletic Field
ASTORIA PARK
Foot Bridge
Playgrounds
Jefferson Park
Franklin High Sch
Our Lady of Mt Carmel Sch
Lincoln Hospital
St Francis Hospital
St Marys Park
St Anns Ch
St Lukes Sch
Gompers Voc High Sch
Dodge Voc High Sch
Immaculate Conception Sch
Mater Chrisi High Sch
Lawrence Cem
Library
St Georges Ch
BRUCKNER BLVD
E 138TH
E 141ST
E 149TH
E 156TH
E 133D
WILLIS
BROOK
ST ANNS
WALNUT AVE
1ST AVE
DRIVE
21ST
23D
24TH
27TH AVE
CRESCENT
31ST
35TH
Playground
PS
JHS
Sta
PO
Fire Sta
278
87
27
E R
R I V E R
E A S T
Hell Gate

Harlem School of the Arts

New York NY 29

645 St. Nicholas Avenue

1974

Ulrich Franzen & Associates

Martin Luther King, Jr. High School 19

New York NY

Amsterdam Avenue & 65th Street

1975

Frost Associates

Sunar Showroom

New York NY 15

730 5th Avenue

1981

Michael Graves

Mobil Building

New York NY 9

150 East 42nd Street

1956

Harrison & Abramovitz

United Nations Headquarters

New York NY 6

United Nations Plaza

1953

Harrison & Abramovitz

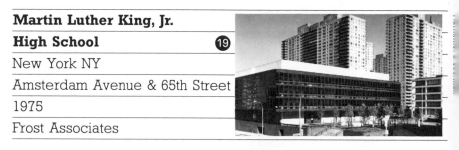

1199 Plaza Coop. Housing

New York NY 27

111th St. & 1st Ave., East Harlem

1975

The Hodne/Stageberg Partners

Norman McGrath

The Museum of Modern Art East Wing 16

New York NY

11 West 53rd Street

1964

Philip Johnson

AT&T Corporate Hdqtrs.

New York NY 14

Madison Avenue & 55th Street

1982

Johnson/Burgee; Simmons Architects

Hedrich-Blessing

Bronx Development Center

New York NY (Bronx) 30

1200 Waters Place

1977

Richard Meier & Associates

Ezra Stoller © Esto

Twin Parks N.E. Housing

New York NY (Bronx) 31

E. 183rd St. & Southern Blvd.

1974

Richard Meier & Associates

Ezra Stoller © Esto

Seagram Building

New York NY 11

375 Park Avenue

1958

Mies van der Rohe

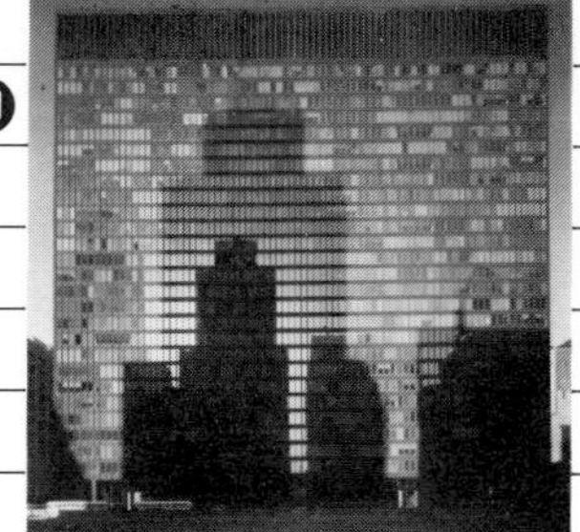

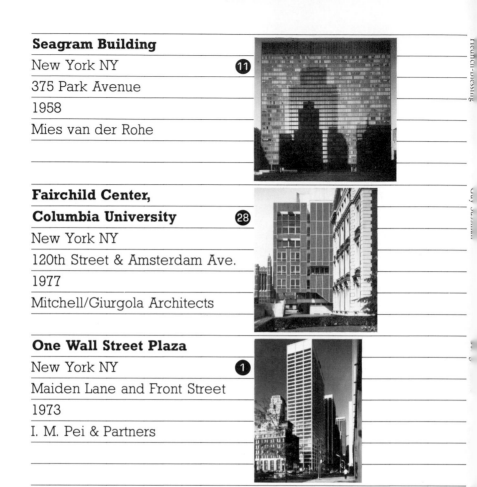

Fairchild Center,
Columbia University 28

New York NY

120th Street & Amsterdam Ave.

1977

Mitchell/Giurgola Architects

One Wall Street Plaza

New York NY 1

Maiden Lane and Front Street

1973

I. M. Pei & Partners

National Airlines Terminal

New York NY 

JFK International Airport

1970

I. M. Pei & Partners

Physical Education Building

New York NY (Brooklyn) 

Kingsborough College

1977

James Stewart Polshek & Partners

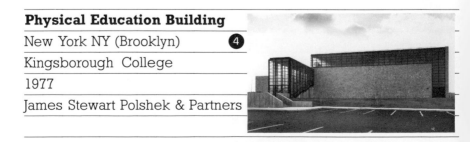

Ford Foundation
New York NY 8
320 East 43rd Street
1968
Kevin Roche John Dinkeloo
& Associates

UN Plaza Hotel & Ofc. Bldg.
New York NY 7
First Avenue & 44th Street
1975
Kevin Roche John Dinkeloo
& Associates

Metropolitan Museum of Art Additions 25
New York NY
Fifth Avenue & 82nd Street
1974 to 1980
Roche Dinkeloo & Associates

Vivian Beaumont Allen Repertory Theater 18
New York NY
Lincoln Center
1964
Eero Saarinen & Associates

David Hirsch

CBS Headquarters
New York NY 17
51 West 52nd Street
1964
Eero Saarinen & Associates

Roche Dinkeloo

TWA Terminal

New York NY 22

JFK International Airport

1962

Eero Saarinen & Associates

Eastwood Apartments

New York NY 

Main Street, Roosevelt Island

1976

Sert Jackson & Associates

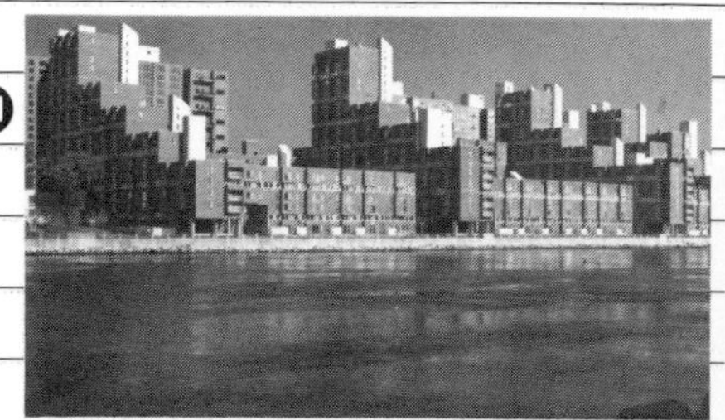

Marine Midland Bank

New York NY 2

140 Broadway

1967

Skidmore Owings & Merrill

Lever House

New York NY 

54th Street & Park Avenue

1952

Skidmore Owings & Merrill

Manufacturers Hanover Trust Company 

New York NY

510 Fifth Avenue

1954

Skidmore Owings & Merrill

Citicorp Center

New York NY 12

One Citicorp Center

1977

Hugh Stubbins & Associates

Edward Jacoby

Guggenheim Museum

New York NY 26

5th Avenue & 89th Street

1959

Frank Lloyd Wright

Kathryn Smith

World Trade Center

New York NY 3

1 World Trade Center

1972

Minoru Yamasaki; Emory Roth

Balthazar Korab

Rainbow Ctr. Winter Garden

Niagara Falls NY

Rainbow Blvd. near La Salle

1977

Gruen Associates

Norman McGrath

The College Center

Plattsburgh NY

State University of New York

1974

Mitchell/Giurgola Architects

Rollin La France

Ferry-Sales Coop. Dormitory
Poughkeepsie NY
Vassar College
1950
Marcel Breuer

H. F. Davis
Powerhouse Theater
Poughkeepsie NY
Vassar College
1973
Robertson Ward

Dormitory, Dining Hall,
Student Union
Purchase NY
State University of New York
1973
Gwathmey Siegel & Associates

First Unitarian Church
Rochester NY
220 South Winton Road
1967
Louis I. Kahn

Administration, Student
Union, Physical Education
Rochester NY
Rochester Institute of Technology
1969
Roche Dinkeloo & Associates

National Technical Institute for the Deaf
Rochester NY
One Lomb Memorial Drive
1974
Hugh Stubbins & Associates

Jonathan Green

Clark House
Southhampton LI NY
Route 274, Shinnecock Hills
1980
Susana Torre

Timothy Hursley/B. Korab

Everson Museum of Art
Syracuse NY
Harrison & South State Streets
1968
I. M. Pei & Partners

Ezra Stoller © Esto

House in Old Westbury
Westbury LI NY
73 Bacon Road
1971
Richard Meier & Associates

Ezra Stoller © Esto

Kislevitz House
Westhampton NY
10 Lott Avenue
1977
Gwathmey Siegel & Associates

Norman McGrath

Gothic Cottage

Woodstock NY

Plochmann Lane

1973

Lester Walker

IBM Research Center

Yorktown Heights NY

Route 134

1961

Eero Saarinen & Associates

New Jersey

AT&T Long Lines Hdqtrs.

Bedminster NJ

Interstate 287 at U.S. 206

1976

John Carl Warnecke & Assoc.

Bell Labs Research Center

Holmdel NJ

Roberts Road

1962

Eero Saarinen & Associates

Stockton State College

Pomona NJ

1971 to Present

Geddes Brecher

Qualls Cunningham

Institute for Advanced Studies

Princeton NJ

Olden Lane, Princeton University

1972

Geddes Brecher

Qualls Cunningham

George Cserna

Graves House

Princeton NJ

44 Patton Avenue

Ongoing

Michael Graves

Thomas & Betts

Corporate Headquarters

Raritan NJ

Route 202

1977

Gwathmey Siegel & Associates

Otto Baitz

Jewish Community Center

Trenton NJ

909 Lower Ferry Road

1959

Louis I. Kahn

Kahn Collection, U of PA

Erdman Hall Dormitories

Bryn Mawr PA

Bryn Mawr College

1965

Louis I. Kahn

Kahn Collection, U of PA

Columbia Bridge
East Park Reservoir
Athletic Field
FAIRMOUNT
EAST
READING
WEST
SCHUYLKILL
RIVER
Water Tank
Memorial Hall
NORMAL
Most Precious
Blaine Sch
Stokley Sch
PENN CENTRAL
RIDGE
25TH
33D
Sartain Sch
Kelley Sch
31ST
MASTER
29TH
27TH
Recreation Center
Kane Sch
Morris Sch
GIRARD COLLEGE
LEIDY
AVE
4 LANE
GIRARD
POPLAR
ST
30
POOL
ELEV
12
PARK
Lemon Hill
ZOO
PARRISH
ASPEN
Hosp
Substa
Hospital
44TH
42D
LANCASTER
39TH
Belmont Sch
McMichael Sch
Gaging Sta
BM 25
St Francis Xaiver Sch
Museum of Art
WALLACE
36TH
34TH
32D
41ST
PRESTON
HAMILTON
13
Locke Sch
Lee Park
POWELTON
RACE
676
76
Fire Sta
PO
Radio Towers (WHAT)
Drexel Institute of Technology
30th St Sta
St James Sch
40TH
UNIVERSITY OF PENNSYLVANIA
B & O Sta
WALNUT
Pillar of Fire Sch
Franklin Field
Penn
Museum
VA HOSPITAL
Clark Park
45TH
Woodlands Cemetery
Convention Hall
SPRUCE
PINE
SOUTH
Wilson Sch
US Naval Home
FITZWATER
Arthur Sch
Peirce Sch
Playgound
10
11
9
8
7

Lincoln Memorial Museum
Gettysburg PA
Battlefield Visitor Center
1963
Richard J. Neutra &
Robert Alexander

Olivetti-Underwood Factory
Harrisburg PA
2800 Valley Road
1970
Louis I. Kahn

Neighborhood Center
Lancaster PA
South Duke Street
1975
Friday Architects/Planners

Armstrong Cork Company Styling and Design Building
Lancaster PA
Columbus Ave. in Tech Center
1971
The Kling Partnership

Old Pine Community Center
Philadelphia PA 1
4th and Lombard Streets
1977
Friday Architects/Planners

Police Headquarters
Philadelphia PA 4
7th and Race Streets
1963
Geddes Brecher
Qualls Cunningham

Lawrence Williams

Richards Medical
Research Laboratory 9
Philadelphia PA
3700 Hamilton Walk, Univ. of PA
1964
Louis I. Kahn

Kahn Collection, U of PA

University Museum,
Academic Wing 8
Philadelphia PA
33rd and Spruce Streets
1971
Mitchell/Giurgola Architects

Rollin La France

United Way Building
Philadelphia PA 6
7 Benjamin Franklin Parkway
1971
Mitchell/Giurgola Architects

Rollin La France

Society Hill Towers
and Townhouses 2
Philadelphia PA
Dock and South Third Streets
1964
I. M. Pei & Partners

Robert Damora

Rittenhouse Swim Club

Philadelphia PA 7

2020 Lombard Street

1961

Schlesinger & Vreeland

Guild House

Philadelphia PA 5

711 Spring Garden Street

1965

Venturi & Rauch;

Cope & Lippincott

Venturi House

Philadelphia PA 10

8330 Millman St., Chestnut Hill

1964

Venturi & Rauch

Franklin Court

Philadelphia PA 3

314–322 Market Street

1976

Venturi Rauch & Scott Brown

Sarah Scaife Gallery,
Carnegie Institute

Pittsburgh PA

4400 Forbes Avenue

1974

Edward Larrabee Barnes Assoc.

U.S. Steel Building

Pittsburgh PA

600 Grant Street

1971

Harrison & Abramovitz

Ezra Stoller © Esto

Alcoa Building

Pittsburgh PA

1501 Allegheny Square

1953

Harrison & Abramovitz

Photo Associates

Faculty Club

University Park PA

Pennsylvania State University

1976

Venturi Rauch & Scott Brown

Tom Bernard

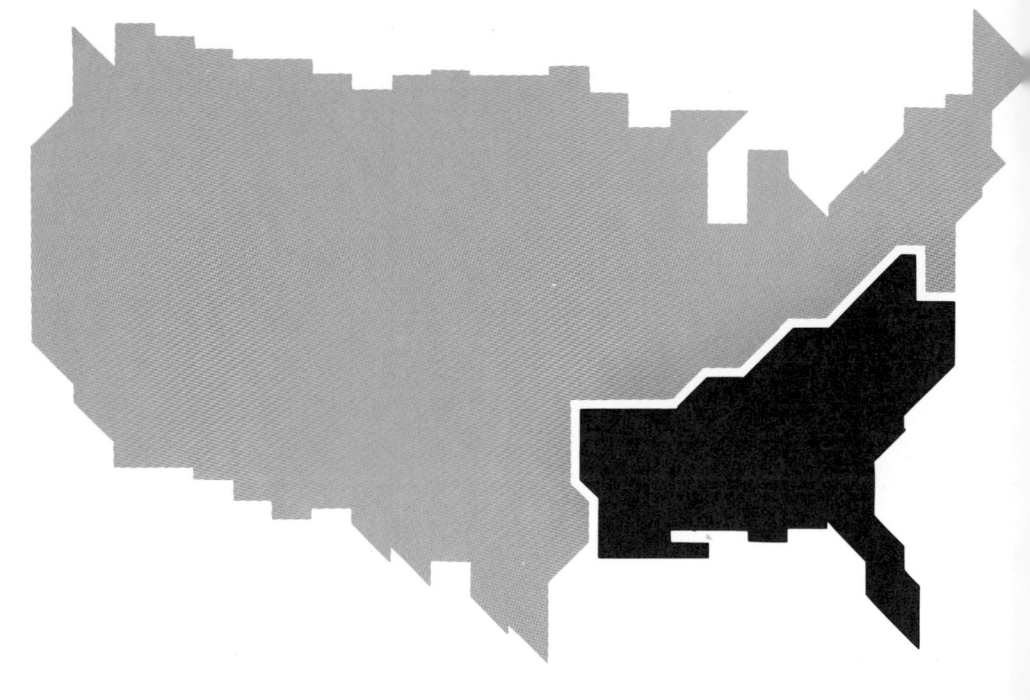

S O U T H E A S T

Morris Mechanic Theater

Baltimore MD

Charles and Baltimore Streets

1967

Johansen & Bhavnani

Coldspring Deck Housing

Baltimore MD

Coldspring New Town

1978

Moshe Safdie & Associates

Waterfront Redevelopment

Baltimore MD

Harborplace

1981

Benjamin Thompson

Comsat Laboratories

Clarksburg MD

22300 Comsat Drive

1969

DMJM

Merriweather Post Pavilion of Music

Columbia MD

Little Patuxent Parkway

1967

Gehry Walsh & O'Malley

Rouse Company Hdqtrs.
Columbia MD
10275 Little Patuxent Parkway
1974
Frank O. Gehry & Associates

Norman McGrath

Oceanfront Condominium
Ocean City MD
Coastal Highway near 96th St.
1976
William Morgan Architects

Robert Lautman

Salisbury School
Salisbury MD
Hobbs Road
1972
Hardy Holzman Pfeiffer Assoc.

Norman McGrath

District of Columbia

HUD Headquarters
Washington DC
7th and D Streets N.W.
1968
Marcel Breuer & Herbert
Beckhard; Nolen/Swinburne

Robert Lautman

Hubert H. Humphrey Bldg.
Washington DC
3rd and Independence S.W.
1976
Marcel Breuer & Herbert
Beckhard; Nolen/Swinburne

Ben Schnall

American Film Institute Headquarters
Washington DC
2700 F St. N.W. (Kennedy Ctr.)
1973
Hardy Holzman Pfeiffer Assoc.

National Permanent Bldg.
Washington DC
1775 Pennsylvania Avenue N.W.
1977
Hartman-Cox Architects

Euram Building
Washington DC
21 DuPont Circle N.W.
1971
Hartman-Cox Architects

Florence Hollis Head Chapel
Washington DC
Mount Vernon College
1970
Hartman-Cox Architects

Nat'l Air & Space Museum
Washington DC
The Mall and
Independence Avenue S.W.
1976
Hellmuth Obata & Kassabaum

Museum for Pre-Columbian Art
Washington DC
1703 32nd Street N.W.
1963
Philip Johnson

Ezra Stoller©Esto

Int'l Monetary Fund Hdqtrs.
Washington DC
700 19th St. N.W.
1973
The Kling Partnership

Tom Crane

National Gallery of Art, East Building
Washington DC
Pennsylvania Ave. & 4th St. S.W.
1978
I. M. Pei & Partners

Ezra Stoller©Esto

Terminal Building
Washington DC (Chantilly VA)
Dulles International Airport
1962
Eero Saarinen & Associates

Ezra Stoller©Esto

Hirshhorn Museum
Washington DC
Independence Avenue and
7th Street S.W.
1974
Skidmore Owings & Merrill

Ezra Stoller©Esto

American Institute of Architects Headquarters

Washington DC

1735 New York Avenue N.W.

1973

The Architects Collaborative

Federal Home Loan Bank

Washington DC

17th and G Streets N.W.

1976

Urbahn Associates

John F. Kennedy Grave

Washington DC (Arlington VA)

Arlington National Cemetery

1965

John Carl Warnecke & Assoc.

Lavinger Memorial Library

Washington DC

Georgetown University

1970

John Carl Warnecke & Assoc.

Washington MTA Stations

Washington DC

41 Stations

1970s

Harry Weese & Associates

Given Estates
Asheville NC
Sweeten Creek Road
1979
William Morgan & Associates;
Moore Robinson Associates

Otto Baitz

Carmel Presbyterian Church
Charlotte NC
Providence Road
1975
Wheatley/Whisnant Architects

Gordon Schenck Jr.

Mecklenburg County Courthouse
Charlotte NC
800 East Fourth Street
1978
Wolf Associates

David Franzen © Esto

North Carolina Nat'l Bank
Charlotte NC
1535 Park Road
1972
Wolf Associates

Gordon Schenck Jr.

Colvard Building
Charlotte NC
University of North Carolina
1979
Wolf Associates

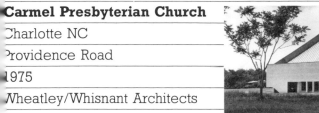

Gordon Schenck Jr.

Equitable Life Assurance Service Center
Charlotte NC
6301 Morrison Boulevard
1977
Wolf Associates

Guilford County Courthouse and Administration Center
Greensboro NC
Government Plaza
1973
Eduardo Catalano

Raleigh House
Raleigh NC
Ridge Rd. near Hillsboro Street
1955
Eduardo Catalano

State Arena
Raleigh NC
No. Carolina State Fairgrounds
1953
Matthew Nowicki

School of Design Addition
Raleigh NC
North Carolina State University
1978
Wolf Associates

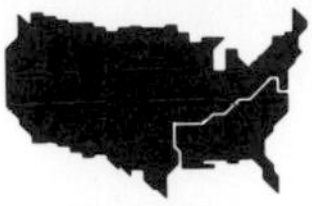

National Humanities Center
Triangle Park NC
Route 40 between Raleigh
and Chapel Hill
1978
Hartman-Cox Architects

Robert Lautman

Burroughs-Wellcome Co. HQ
Triangle Park NC
Route 40 between Raleigh
and Chapel Hill
1972
Paul Rudolph

Joseph Molitor

Tennessee

Hunter Museum of Art
Chattanooga TN
10 Bluff View Avenue
1975
Derthick & Henley

Otto Baitz

Temple Israel
Memphis TN
1376 East Massey Road
1976
Gassner Nathan & Partners

Otto Baitz

Commercial and Industrial Bank
Memphis TN
200 Madison Avenue
1972
Gassner Nathan Browne

Otto Baitz

Hyatt Regency Ridgeway
Memphis TN
939 Ridge Lake Boulevard
1975
Walk Jones & Francis Mah

South Carolina

The Treetops
Hilton Head SC
Cordillo Pkwy. near Pope Ave.
1974
Stoller/Glasser & Marquis Assoc.

Georgia

Peachtree Center
Atlanta GA
225 Peachtree Street N.E.
1967
John Portman & Associates

Omni International
Atlanta GA
One Omni International
1975
Ventulett Thompson Stainback & Associates

Florida

Dunehouse
Atlantic Beach FL
1941 Oceanfront
1975
William Morgan Architects

Morgan House
Atlantic Beach FL
1945 Oceanfront
1973
William Morgan Architects

Ronald Thomas

Vehicle Assembly and Launch Control Facility
Cape Canaveral FL
1967
URSAM (Urbahn Assoc. et al)

Federal Building–U.S. Courthouse
Fort Lauderdale FL
Broward Boulevard
1979
William Morgan Architects

Robert Lautman

Florida State Museum
Gainesville FL
University of Florida
1970
William Morgan Architects;
Forrest M. Kelley

Police Memorial Building
Jacksonville FL
501 East Bay Street
1975
William Morgan Architects

Otto Baitz

Disney World Hotel
Orlando FL
Walt Disney World
1972
Welton Becket Associates

Riverview H.S. Library
Sarasota FL
Ramway Drive
1972
Frank Folsom Smith & Partners
(James Durden, Design Assoc.)

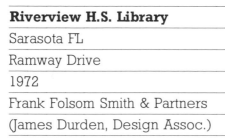

Siesta Key Chapel
Sarasota FL
Gleason Blvd. and Ocean Blvd.
Completion date unknown
Frank Folsom Smith & Partners
(James Durden, Design Assoc.)

Penthouse on the Lake
Sarasota FL
Sandy Cove Village
1968
Frank Folsom Smith & Partners
(James Durden, Design Assoc.)

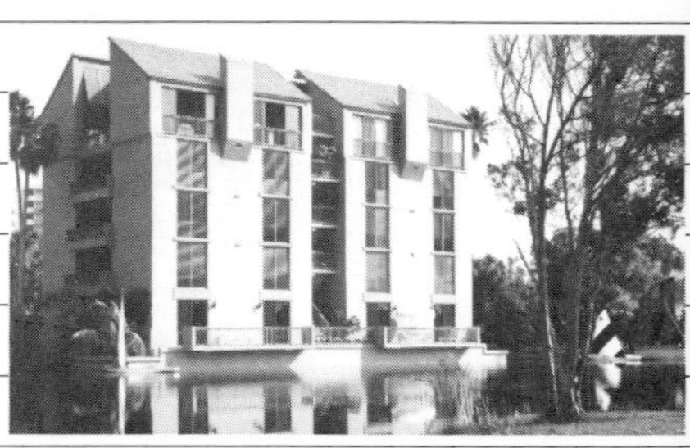

Alabama

Civic Center
Birmingham AL
9th Avenue & 19th Street
1977
Geddes Brecher
Qualls Cunningham

St. Patrick's Church and Catholic Center

Robertsdale AL

State Hwy. 59 near Illinois Street

1974

Blitch Architects, Inc.

Franz Lotz Miller

Mississippi

Biloxi Library & Cultural Ctr.

Biloxi MS

Lameuse and Delauney Streets

1977

MLTW/Turnbull Associates

Morley Baer

Louisiana

Piazza d'Italia

New Orleans LA

Lafayette Mall

1978

August Perez Associates; Charles Moore, Urban Innovations Group

Norman McGrath

Arkansas

Thorncrown Chapel

Eureka Springs AR

Highway 62

1980

Fay Jones & Associates

Horsley & Lark

Pallone House

Little Rock AR

Garrison Rd. & Jones Loop

1976

Fay Jones & Associates

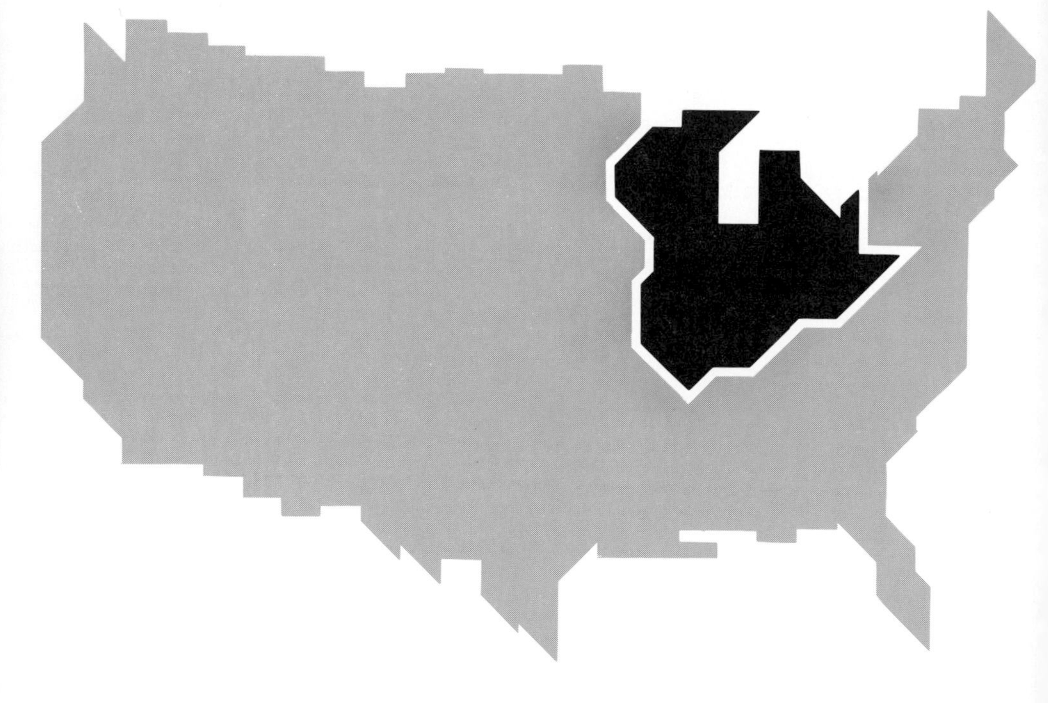

M I D E A S T

Student Union Building
Cleveland OH
Cleveland State University
1974
Don M. Hisaka & Associates

George Cserna

Thwing Center
Cleveland OH
Case Western Reserve University
1980
Don M. Hisaka & Associates

Thom Abel

Park Synagogue and Community Center
Cleveland OH
3300 Mayfield Road
1952
Eric Mendelsohn

Walter C. Leedy Jr.

Beachwood Place
Cleveland OH
26300 Cedar Road
1978
RTKL

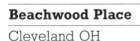

Richard Anderson

School of Art
Kent OH
Kent State University
1970
John Andrews

Allen Memorial Art Museum
Oberlin OH
Oberlin College
1976
Venturi Rauch & Scott Brown

Tom Bernard

Raymon H. Mulford Library
Toledo OH
Medical College of Ohio
1975
Don M. Hisaka & Associates

George Cserna

Power Center for the Performing Arts
Ann Arbor MI
University of Michigan
1971
Roche Dinkeloo & Associates

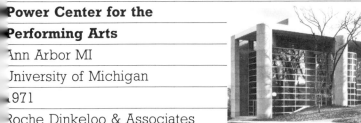

IBM Southfield Centre
Detroit MI (Southfield)
8000 Nine Mile Rd.
1979
Gunnar Birkerts & Associates

Balthazar Korab

The Calvary Baptist Church
Detroit MI
000 McDougall Avenue
1978
Gunnar Birkerts & Associates

Northland Shopping Center

Detroit MI
Southfield
1954
Gruen Associates

Detroit Science Center

Detroit MI
5020 John R Street
1978
William Kessler & Associates

Center for Creative Studies

Detroit MI
245 East Kirby Street
1976
William Kessler & Associates

Detroit Receiving Hospital

Detroit MI
4201 St. Antoine Street
1980
William Kessler; Zeidler Partnership; Giffels Associates

McGregor Memorial Community Conference Ctr.

Detroit MI
Wayne State University
1958
Minoru Yamasaki & Associates

Temple Emanuel
Grand Rapids MI
1715 East Fulton
1953
Eric Mendelsohn

Upjohn Company
Kalamazoo MI
7000 Portage Road
1961
Skidmore Owings & Merrill

Ezra Stoller©Esto

St. Francis de Sales Church
Muskegon MI
McCracken Street
1966
Marcel Breuer and
Herbert Beckhard

Hedrich-Blessing

General Motors Tech. Ctr.
Warren MI
Twelve Mile and Mound Roads
1956
Eero Saarinen & Associates

Ezra Stoller©Esto

Herman Miller Headquarters
Zeeland MI
8500 Byron Road
1976
A. Quincy Jones & Associates

W. D. Richards Elem. School

Columbus IN

3311 Fairlawn

1964

Edward Larrabee Barnes;

Thomas Dorste

Lincoln Elementary School

Columbus IN

Fifth Street

1967

Gunnar Birkerts & Associates

Indiana Bell Switching Ofc.

Columbus IN

Franklin and Seventh

1978

Caudill Rowlett Scott

Fodrea Community School

Columbus IN

2775 Illinois

1974

Caudill Rowlett Scott;

A. Dean Taylor

The Commons and Courthouse Center

Columbus IN

302 Washington Street

1974

Gruen Associates

Occupational Health Center
Columbus IN
605 Cottage Street
1973
Hardy Holzman Pfeiffer Assoc.

Norman McGrath

L. Frances Smith Elementary School
Columbus IN
4505 Waycross
1970
Johansen & Bhavnani

Balthazar Korab

Columbus East Senior High School
Columbus IN
230 South Marr Road
1972
Mitchell/Giurgola Architects

Rollin La France

Southside Junior High School
Columbus IN
State Rd. 58 near U.S. 31A
1969
Eliot Noyes

Balthazar Korab

Cleo Rogers Memorial County Library
Columbus IN
5th St. betw. Franklin & Lafayette
1970
I. M. Pei & Partners

Balthazar Korab

Quinco Consulting Center
Columbus IN
25th Street & Highway 31
1970
James Stewart Polshek & Partners

Irwin Union Bank & Trust Co.
Columbus IN
5th St. at Washington & Jackson
1972
Kevin Roche John Dinkeloo
& Associates

United States Post Office
Columbus IN
Jackson and 4th Streets
1969
Kevin Roche John Dinkeloo
& Associates

North Christian Church
Columbus IN
Tipton Lane
1962
Eero Saarinen & Associates

Irwin Union Bank & Trust
Columbus IN
5th St. at Washington & Jackson
1956
Eero Saarinen & Associates

The Republic Newspapor Plant
Columbus IN
333 2nd Street
1971
Skidmore Owings & Merrill

Ezra Stoller©Esto

Parkside Elementary School
Columbus IN
1400 Parkside Drive
1960
The Architects Collaborative

Fire Station No. 4
Columbus IN
4730 25th Street
1968
Venturi & Rauch

Mabel McDowell Elementary School
Columbus IN
2700 McKinley Avenue
1962
John Carl Warnecke & Assoc.

First Baptist Church
Columbus IN
3300 Fairlawn Drive
1965
Harry Weese & Associates

Balthazar Korab

Clowes Memorial
Symphony Hall
Indianapolis IN
Butler University Campus
1964
Johansen & Bhavnani

George Cserna

College Life Insurance
Company of America
Indianapolis IN
3500 DePauw Boulevard
1971
Roche Dinkeloo & Associates

Shrine (Roofless Church)
New Harmony IN
420 North Street
1960
Philip Johnson

The Atheneum
New Harmony IN
300 North Street
1979
Richard Meier & Associates

Cummins Engine Co. Plant
Walesboro IN
I-65 and 450 South
1973
Kevin Roche John Dinkeloo
& Associates

Kentucky Power Co. Hdqtrs.

Ashland KY

Central Avenue

1976

Kevin Roche John Dinkeloo & Associates

Jerrico Corporate Hdqtrs.

Lexington KY

101 Jerrico Drive

1978

Bennet & Tune

Barbara Elliott Martin

Riverfront Plaza/Belvedere

Louisville KY

One Riverfront Plaza

1973

Doxiadis Associates; Jasper Ward; Lawrence Melillo

Ford House

Aurora IL

404 South Edgelawn

1950

Bruce Goff

Philip Welch

Humanities & Soc. Sci. Ctr.

Carbondale IL

Southern Illinois University

1975

Geddes Brecher Qualls Cunningham

George Cserna

Logan Sch
Goethe Sch
26
25
24
23
Holstein Park
ELSTON
Thomas Sch
CLYBOURN
Alexian Hospital
Mayer Sch
Sta
Headley Sch
RAPID
AVE
598
KENNEDY
Pulaski Sch
se Sch
593
BM 590
Sta
St Th Conve
Adams Park
597
Sta
ST
AVE
AVE
Drummond Sch
St Mary of the Angels Convent
AND
PACIFIC
ST
WOOD
WESTERN
AVE
Annunciation Sch
Burr Sch
wood Park
64
N
BM 599
Sta
593
Turning Basin
BM 593
NORTH BR
St Aloysius Sch
St Josephinum High Sch
W LEMOYNE ST
Kosciuszko Sch
St Elizabeth Hospital
Sabin Sch
Wicker Park
Dean Playground
Von Humboldt Sch
Wicker Park Sch
AVE
Pulaski Park
Tuley High Sch
N
ROCKWELL
POTOMAC
AVE
AVE
Schley Sch
PO
596
ST
ST
W
DIVISION
BLVD
S
AVE
EXPRESSWAY
Andersen Sch
Holy Trinity High Sch
St Marks Sch
CAMPBELL
6 LANE
St Mary of Nazareth Hospital
ST
N
ayette
St Helens Sch
W
AUGUSTA
ST
Wells High Sch
BLVD
Peabody Sch
Columbus Sch
NOBLE
N
W
IOWA
ST
AVE
BM 605
Chopin Sch
601
St Nicholas Sch
Commercial Park
Eckhart Park
N
22
596
W
CHI
Motley Sch
OAKLEY
LEAVITT
W
HOYNE
HURON
WOOD
PAULINA
ST
N
594
Carpenter Sch
Smith Park
Talcott Sch
ST
ASHLAND
Bickerdike Sq Park
W
OHIO
WOLCOTT
St Columbkille Sch
OGDEN
Mitchell Sch
Otis Sch
W
GRAND
N
N
N
DAMEN
593
ST
CHICAGO
AND
NORTH WESTERN
W
KINZIE
CHICAGO
MILWAUKEE
ST PAUL
AND
PACIFIC
W
FULTON
N
N
N
ST
N
N
6 LANE
RACINE
Sta
RAPID
TRANSIT
Dett Sch
LAKE
ST
Spalding Sch
Union Park
4 LANE
N
W
W
RAND
Suder Sch
Birney Sch
595
4 LANE
BLVD
4 LANE
WASH
N
WARREN
595
BLVD
Chicago Stadium
Brown Sch
W
MADISON
Sain Park
Herbert Sch
W
MONROE
Grant Sch
Rockwell Park
McKinley Sch
34
66
Skinner Park
Skinner Sch
6 LA
N
W
ADAMS
C & NW
Touhy Park
6 LANE
Jo Sc
W
JACKS
Chicago Jr College (Crane Branch)
EXPRESSWAY
Sta

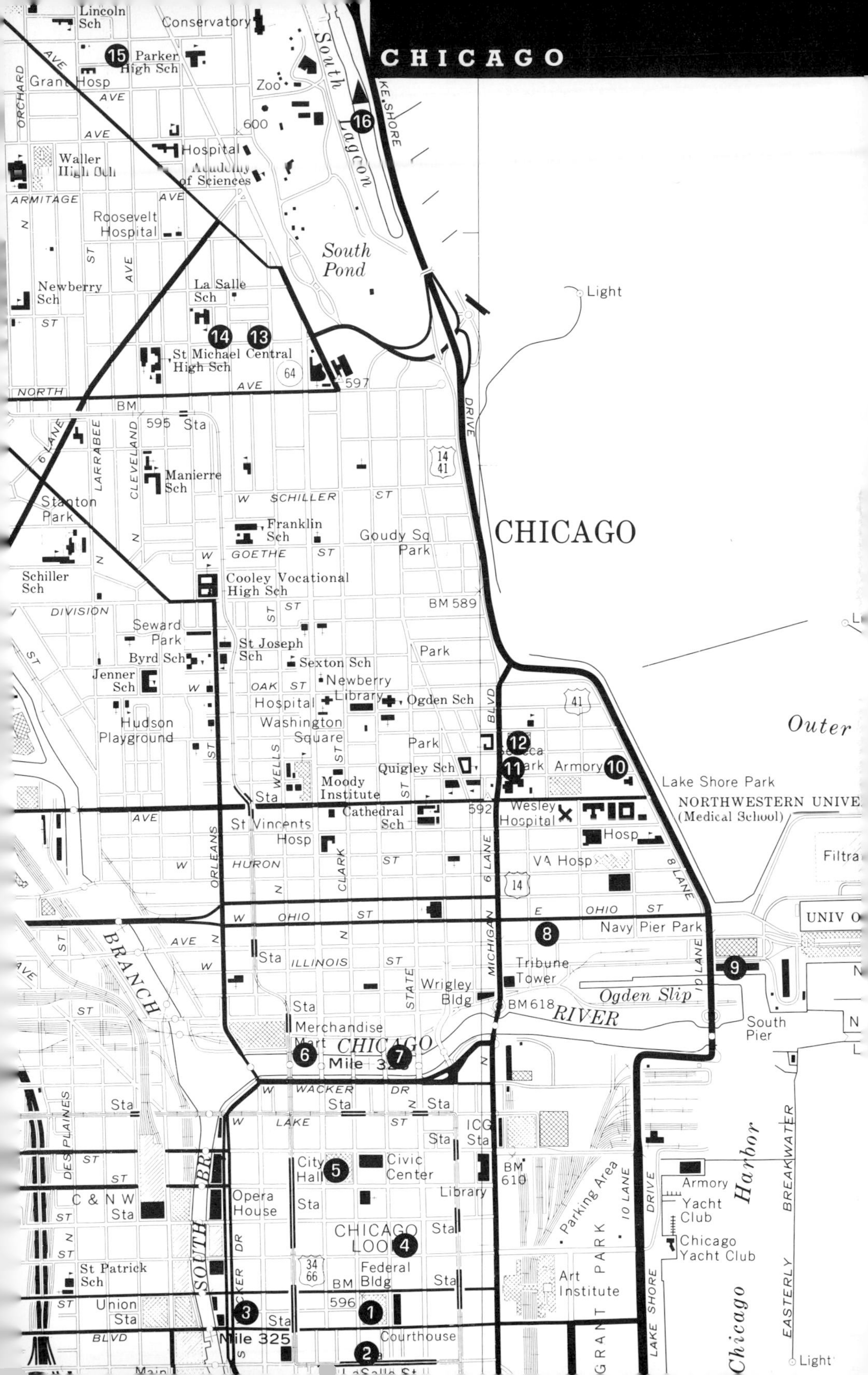
Lincoln Sch
Conservatory
South Lagoon
Parker High Sch
Grant Hosp
Zoo
Lake Shore Drive
Orchard
Ave
600
Hospital
Waller High Sch
Academy of Sciences
Armitage Ave
Roosevelt Hospital
South Pond
Newberry Sch
La Salle Sch
Light
14
13
St Michael Central High Sch
64
597
North Ave
BM 595
Sta
6 Lane
Larrabee
Cleveland
Manierre Sch
Drive
14
41
Stanton Park
W Schiller St
Franklin Sch
Goudy Sq Park
CHICAGO
Schiller Sch
W Goethe St
Cooley Vocational High Sch
Division
BM 589
Seward Park
St Joseph Sch
Byrd Sch
Jenner Sch
Sexton Sch
Park
Oak St
Newberry Library
Hospital
Ogden Sch
41
Hudson Playground
Washington Square
Outer
Park
12
Seneca Park
Quigley Sch
11
Armory
10
Wells
Moody Institute
Lake Shore Park
Sta
592
Wesley Hospital
Northwestern University (Medical School)
Ave
Cathedral Sch
St Vincents Hosp
Hosp
Filtra
W Huron St
Clark
VA Hosp
8 Lane
Orleans
6 Lane
14
W Ohio St
E Ohio St
Navy Pier Park
Univ O
8
Branch
Michigan
Ave
Sta
Illinois St
Tribune Tower
10 Lane
9
State
Wrigley Bldg
BM 618
Ogden Slip
River
Sta
South Pier
Merchandise Mart
Chicago
6
7
Mile 327
W Wacker Dr
Sta
Des Plaines
W Lake St
ICG Sta
Sta
St
City Hall
5
Civic Center
BM 610
Parking Area
10 Lane
Drive
Armory
Yacht Club
Harbor
Breakwater
C & N W Sta
Opera House
Library
St
Sta
Chicago Yacht Club
Chicago Loop
4
South Br
St Patrick Sch
34
66
Federal Bldg
BM 596
Art Institute
Grant Park
Lake Shore
Easterly
Chicago
Union Sta
3
1
Sta
Blvd
Mile 325
Courthouse
2
Light

HARRISON
Campbell Park
King Sch
Irving Sch
4 LANE
6 LANE
McLaren Sch
Vernon Park
Hospital
Medical Center
Sheridan Park
Jacks
TAYLOR
St Mary High Sch
Hosp
Jefferson Sch
Riis Sch
ROOSEVELT
BM 592
BM 591
Montefiore Sch
Fire Sta
Gladstone Sch
Allen Sch
Fosco Playground
Medill Sch
Sta
4 LANE
B & O C T
B N
Jirka Sch
St Procopius High Sch
18TH
St Ann High Sch
Harrison Park
DAMEN
Cooper Sch
PO
LOOMIS
RACINE
19TH
Komensky Sch
Sta
St Pius High Sch
21 ST
Pickard Sch
CERMAK
C B & Q
BLUE ISLAND
Whittier Sch
Lithuanian Sch
WESTERN
SOUTH
Turning Basin
HILLOCK
BM
St Barbara High Sch
4 LANE
LAYMAN
BM 594
Holden High Sch
CANAL
EXPRESSWAY
BM 592
ASHLAND
St Mary High Sch
33D
FORK
Hoyne Playground
34TH
Everett Sch
BM 593
ILLINOIS CENTRAL GULF
35TH
B & O C T
Longfellow Sch
WOOD
Green Sch
Burroughs Sch
36TH
St Maurice Sch
37TH
St Andrews Sch

CHICAGO
Customhouse
Breakwater
Shedd Aquarium
NATURAL HISTORY MUSEUM
SOLDIER FIELD
Burnham Park Harbor
MEIGS FIELD
Park
Mile 324
CHICAGO RIVER
Hospital
Chicago Technical College
E CERMAK RD
McCormick Place
Haines Sch
Mercy Hospital
Williams Sch
Sheridan Sch
Ward Sch
St Anthony Sch
McGuane Park
Healy Sch
Drake Sch
Dunbar High Sch
Reese Hospital
Trinity Sch
St David Sch
Douglas Sch
Ill Institute of Technology
Chicago Institute of Technology
Armour Park
De La Salle Institute
Comiskey Park
Sanitarium
Doolittle Sch
McClellan Sch
Ellis Park
Abbott Sch
Raymond Sch
Mayo Sch
Madden Park
Nativity of Our Lord
DAN RYAN
ROCK ISLAND
PENN CENTRAL
BURNHAM
ILLINOIS CENTRAL
KENNEDY EXPRESSWAY
WABASH AVE
STATE ST
17
18
19
20

Chicago Botanic Gardens

Adm. and Visitors Center 

Chicago IL (Glencoe)

Lake Cook Road

1976

Edward Larrabee Barnes Assoc.

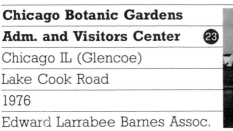

Community Center/

Freedom Hall 

Chicago IL (Park Forest)

410 Lakewood Boulevard

1976

Booth Nagle & Hartray Assoc.

Portals at Grant Place

Chicago IL 

410 West Grant Place

1973

Booth Nagle & Hartray Assoc.

David's Plaza

Chicago IL 

N. Eugenie and N. Wells Streets

1978

Booth Nagle & Hartray Assoc.

House on Lake Michigan

Chicago IL (Glencoe) 

1 Rockgate Terr.

1976

Booth Nagle & Hartray Assoc.

Marina City Apartments

Chicago IL 7

300 North State Street

1964

Bertrand Goldberg & Associates

Hedrich-Blessing

Sunar Furniture Showroom

Chicago IL 6

The Merchandise Mart

1979

Michael Graves

Water Tower Place

Chicago IL 11

845 North Michigan Avenue

1976

Loebl Schlossman Dart & Hackl;

C. F. Murphy

Hedrich-Blessing

Metallurgical Research Bldg.

Chicago IL 18

Illinois Institute of Technology

1946

Mies van der Rohe

Crown Hall

Chicago IL 19

Illinois Institute of Technology

1956

Mies van der Rohe

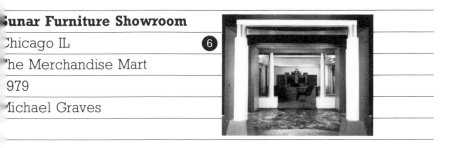

Hedrich-Blessing

Lake Shore Drive Apts.

Chicago IL 10

860-80 N. Lake Shore Drive

1951

Mies van der Rohe; Pace Assoc.

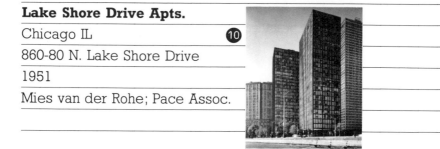

Federal Center

Chicago IL 

230 South Dearborn

1969

Mies van der Rohe;
Schmidt Garden Erickson

McCormick Place

Chicago IL 

South Lake Shore Dr. & 23rd St.

1970

C. F. Murphy Associates

Richard J. Daley Center

Chicago IL 

Clark and Randolph Streets

1966

C. F. Murphy Associates

Hyatt Regency Hotel, O'Hare

Chicago IL 

9300 Bryn Mawr Avenue

1971

John Portman & Associates

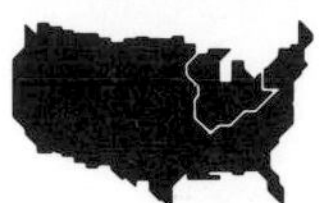

Lake Point Tower

Chicago IL 9

505 North Lake Shore Drive

1968

Schipporeit-Heinrich Associates;
Graham, Anderson, Probst & White

Bob Porth/Hedrich-Blessing

John Hancock Center

Chicago IL 12

875 North Michigan Avenue

1970

Skidmore Owings & Merrill

Ezra Stoller © Esto

Inland Steel Building

Chicago IL 4

30 West Monroe Street

1958

Skidmore Owings & Merrill

Ezra Stoller © Esto

Sears Tower

Chicago IL 3

233 South Wacker Drive

1974

Skidmore Owings & Merrill

Ezra Stoller © Esto

Regional Library for Blind

Chicago IL

1055 West Roosevelt Road 21

1978

Stanley Tigerman & Associates/
City of Chicago

Howard Kaplan

Ukrainian Institute of Modern Art 22

Chicago IL

Chicago and Western Avenues

1977

Stanley Tigerman

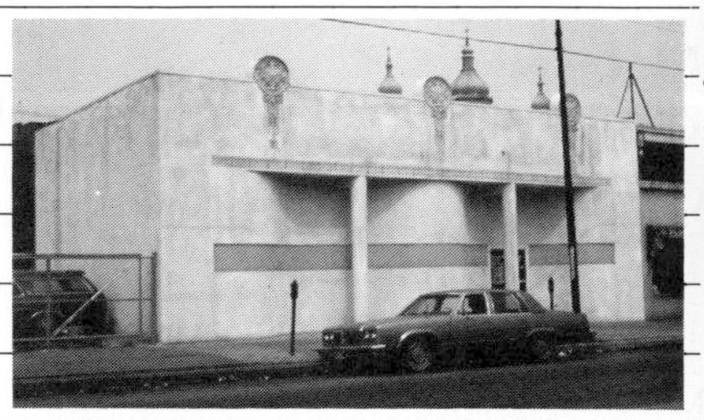

Boardwalk

Chicago IL 16

4343 North Clarendon

1974

Stanley Tigerman

William J. Campbell Courthouse Annex 2

Chicago IL

Clark Street and Van Buren

1975

Harry Weese & Associates

Time-Life Building

Chicago IL 8

541 North Fairbanks Court

1968

Harry Weese & Associates

Eugenie Lane Apartments

Chicago IL 14

N. Eugenie St. & N. Park Ave.

1962

Harry Weese & Associates

North Shore

Congregation Israel 25

Chicago IL (Glencoe)

1185 Sheridan Road

1964

Minoru Yamasaki & Associates

Hecrich-Blessing

Religious Center

Edwardsville IL

Southern Illinois University

1971

Fuller & Sadao

(R. Buckminster Fuller)

Fuller Archives

Deere & Company

West Office Building

Moline IL

John Deere Road

1979

Roche Dinkeloo & Associates

Deere & Company

Headquarters

Moline IL

John Deere Road

1963

Eero Saarinen & Associates

Ezra Stoller ©Esto

Farnsworth House

Plano IL

1950

Mies van der Rohe

Hedrich-Blessing

Aid Association for Lutherans Headquarters

Appleton WI

4321 North Ballard Road

1977

John Carl Warnecke & Assoc.

St. Benedict's Abbey

Green Bay WI (Bennet Lake)

North Avenue & Nelson Road

1972

Stanley Tigerman

Milwaukee Center for the Performing Arts

Milwaukee WI

929 North Water Street

1970

Harry Weese & Associates

S. C. Johnson & Company Research Tower

Racine WI

1525 Howe Street

1951

Frank Lloyd Wright

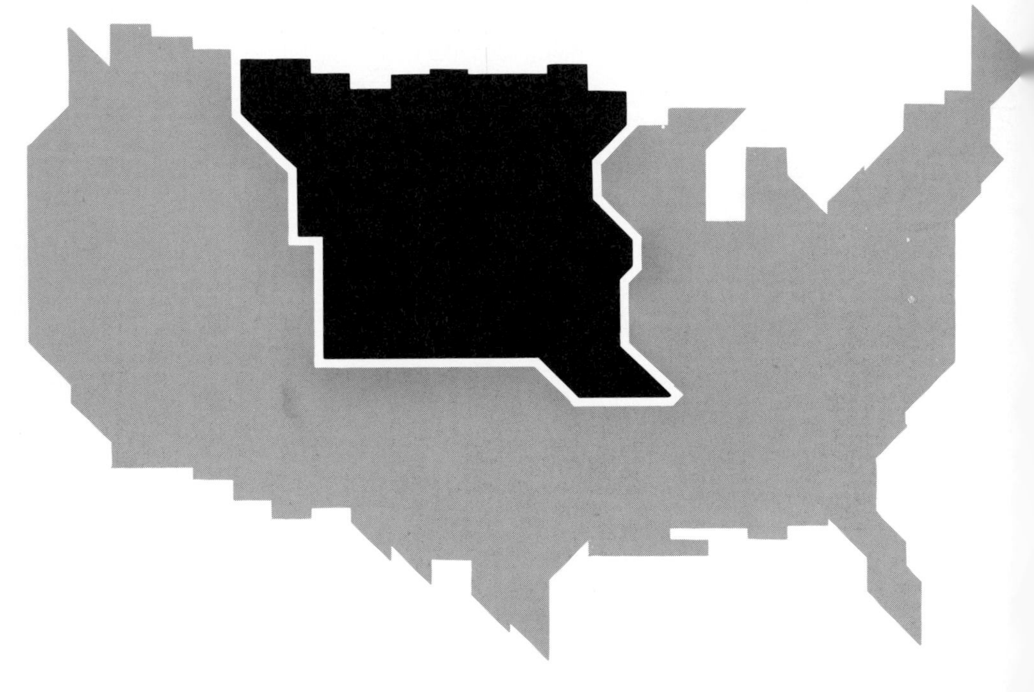

M I D W E S T

St. John's Abbey Church
Collegeville MN
90 miles N.W. of Minneapolis
1961
Marcel Breuer;
Hamilton Smith, Associate

Duluth Public Library
Duluth MN
520 West Superior Street
1980
Gunnar Birkerts & Associates

Walker Art Center
Minneapolis MN
Vineland Place
1971
Edward Larrabee Barnes Assoc.

Federal Reserve Bank
Minneapolis MN
250 Marquette Avenue
1973
Gunnar Birkerts & Associates

Williamson Hall
Minneapolis MN
University of Minnesota
1980
BRW Architects
(Myers & Bennett)

Minneapolis Orchestra Hall
Minneapolis MN
1111 Nicolet Mall
1974
Hardy Holzman Pfeiffer Assoc.;
Hammel Green & Abrahamson

Norman McGrath

Minneapolis Regional Native American Center
Minneapolis MN
1530 Franklin Avenue East
1975
The Hodne/Stageberg Partners

I.D.S. Center
Minneapolis MN
Nicolett Mall
1973
Johnson/Burgee;
Edward F. Baker Associates

Richard Payne

Tyrone Guthrie Theater
Minneapolis MN
725 Vineland Place
1964
Ralph Rapson & Associates

Cedar Square West
Minneapolis MN
1929 South Fifth Street
1974
Ralph Rapson & Associates

Charles A. Schmid

Christ Lutheran Church

Minneapolis MN

3244 34th Avenue South

1949

Eliel & Eero Saarinen

Hennepin County Government Center

Minneapolis MN

2300 Government Center

1976

John Carl Warnecke & Assoc.

Mt. Zion Temple and Community Center

St. Paul MN

1300 Summit Avenue

1954

Eric Mendelsohn

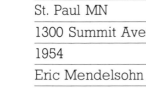

Iowa

Uni-Dome

Cedar Falls IO

University of Northern Iowa

1976

Thorson Brom Broshar Snyder

Capital City State Bank

Des Moines IO

5700 Hickman Road

1972

Charles Herbert & Associates

New Melleray Abbey

Dubuque IO

Country Site near Dubuque

1976

Frank Kacmarcik;

Hammel Green & Abrahamson

Les Tamau

Home State Bank

Jefferson IO

Highway 4 and Central Avenue

1974

Charles Herbert & Associates

Tri-Center

Elementary School

Neola IO

Highway 191, 4 mi. N.E. of Neola

1979

Dana Larson Roubal & Assoc.

Missouri

Freeman House

Joplin MO

Tabor Woods

1957

Bruce Goff

H. Roe Bartle Exhibition Hall

Kansas City MO

Central and 13th Street

1976

C. F. Murphy Associates

Crown Center Hotel

Kansas City MO

1 Pershing Road

1973

Harry Weese & Associates

First Christian Church

Kirksville MO

Harrison and High Streets

1971

Anselevicius/Rupe/Associates

Communications Workers of America Offices

St. Louis MO

2334 Olive Street

1970

Anselevicius/Rupe/Associates

Christ Episcopal Church

St. Louis MO

912 South Beach Boulevard

1971

Blitch Architects

McDonnell Planetarium

St. Louis MO

Forest Park

1962

Hellmuth Obata & Kassabaum

B'nai Amoona Synagogue and Community Center

St. Louis MO

Villa Ridge

1950

Eric Mendelsohn

Jefferson National Expansion Memorial Arch

St. Louis MO

Mark Twain Expressway

1964

Eero Saarinen & Associates

Arteaga Photos

Law School & Soc. Sci. Bldgs.

St. Louis MO

Washington University

1971

Schnebli, Anselevicius & Montgomery

Robert Pettus

Dymaxion Dwelling Machine

Wichita KS

1974 East Street

1945

R. Buckminster Fuller

Fuller Archives

McKnight Art Center and Ulrich Museum of Art

Wichita KS

Wichita State University

1974

Charles F. McAfee, FAIA

Hossain/Unruh

Nebraska

Orpheum Theater Renovation

Omaha NE

409 South 16th Street

1975

Leo A. Daly

Douglas County Correctional Center

Omaha NE

710 South 17th Street

1979

Dana Larson Roubal & Assoc.

North Branch Library

Omaha NE

29th Street & Ames Avenue

1972

Dana Larson Roubal & Associates

South Dakota

Piya Wiconi Community College

Kyle SD

1981

The Hodne/Stageberg Partners

Wyoming

Jackson Hole Information Center

Jackson Hole WY

532 North Cache

1974

Corbett/Associates

National Center for Atmospheric Research

Boulder CO

1850 Table Mesa Drive

1966

I. M. Pei & Partners

Ezra Stoller © Esto

Chapel

Colorado Springs CO

U.S. Air Force Academy

1962

Skidmore Owings & Merrill

Gary Operating Co. Offices

Denver CO

I-25 & County Line Road

1980

Cabel Childress Architects

Cherry Creek Reservoir Picnic Shells

Denver CO

Parker Road and I-225

1972

Cabell Childress; R. Behrens

Boettcher Concert Hall

Denver CO

50 13th Street

1978

Hardy Holzman Pfeiffer Assoc.

Norman McGrath

Park Central
Denver CO
16th and Arapahoe Streets
1973
Muchow Associates

Julius Shulman

Mile High Center
Denver CO
Broadway at 17th Street
1955
I. M. Pei & Partners

Ezra Stoller©Esto

Denver Art Museum
Denver CO
100 West 14th Avenue Parkway
1971
Gio Ponti; James Sudler Assoc.

Rush McCoy

Denver Center Theater Complex
Denver CO
1050 13th Street
1979
Roche Dinkeloo & Associates

Johns-Manville World Headquarters
Denver CO
12999 Dear Creek Canyon Road
1976
The Architects Collaborative

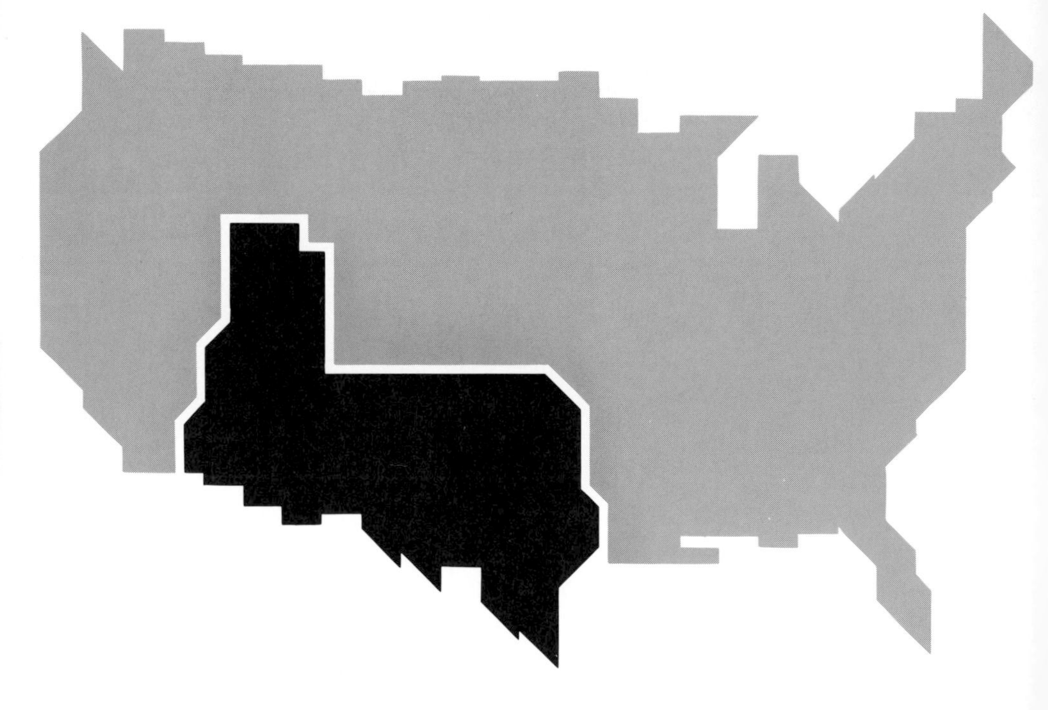

S O U T H W E S T

Price Tower
Bartlesville OK
N.E. 6th Street & Dewey Avenue
1956
Frank Lloyd Wright

Redeemer Lutheran Church Education Building
Bartlesville OK
1100 S.E. Ridgewood Drive
1959
Bruce Goff

Dace House
Beaver OK
1228 Third Street
1964
Bruce Goff

Bavinger House
Norman OK
730 60th Avenue N.E.
1950
Bruce Goff

Greene House
Norman OK
48th Avenue between Robinson and Alameda
1961
Herb Greene

Pollock House

Oklahoma City OK

2400 N.W. 59th

1958

Bruce Goff

Oklahoma Theater Center

Oklahoma City OK

400 West Sheridan

1970

Johansen & Bhavnani

Balthazar Korab

House of the Century

Angleton TX

Route 580

1973

Ant Farm: Richard Jost,
Chip Lord, Doug Michels

Richard Jost

Hyatt Regency Hotel

Dallas TX

Reunion Boulevard

1979

Welton Becket Associates

Balthazar Korab

Texas Instruments Company

Dallas TX

13500 N. Central Expressway

1959

O'Neill Ford & Richard Colley

Eisenberg House
Dallas TX
9624 Rockbrook
1958
Harwell Hamilton Harris

First Unitarian Church
Dallas TX
Preston Road at Normandy
1963
Harwell Hamilton Harris;
David Barrow; Beran & Shelmire

Dallas/Fort Worth Airport
Dallas-Fort Worth TX
Highway 183
1973
Hellmuth Obata & Kassabaum

Dallas Centre, Phase I
Dallas TX
Bryan betw. Harwood & St. Paul
1979
I. M. Pei & Partners

Dallas City Hall
Dallas TX
Young St. betw. Akard & Ervay
1978
I. M. Pei & Partners

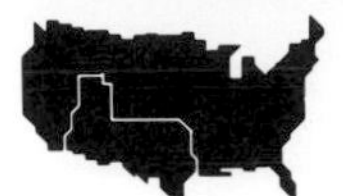

Greenwood Mausoleum
Fort Worth TX
3100 White Settlement Road
1959
Harwell Hamilton Harris

Kimbell Art Museum
Fort Worth TX
1101 Will Rogers Road
1972
Louis I. Kahn

Ezra Stoller © Esto

Hendley Building
Galveston TX
2016 The Strand
1980
Taft Architects

Rothko Chapel
Houston TX
1404 Sul Ross
1971
Howard Barnstone, FAIA &
Eugene Aubry, FAIA

Rick Gardner

Contemporary Arts Museum
Houston TX
5216 Montrose Blvd.
1972
Gunnar Birkerts & Associates

Balthazar Korab

CRS Office Building

Houston TX

1111 West Loop South

1969

Caudill Rowlett Scott

Alley Theater

Houston TX

615 Texas Avenue

1965

Ulrich Franzen & Associates

The Galleria

Houston TX

Westheimer Blvd. nr. S. Post Oak

1978

Hellmuth Obata & Kassabaum

Pennzoil Place

Houston TX

Milam & Louisiana

1976

Johnson/Burgee

Post Oak Central III

Houston TX

Post Oak Road

1981

Johnson/Burgee;

Fitzgerald Associates

Indeterminate Facade
Houston TX
Kingspoint & Kleckley Streets
1975
SITE

Tenneco Building
Houston TX
1010 Milam
1963
Skidmore Owings & Merrill

Tranquility Park
Houston TX
500 Walker Street
1979
Charles Tapley Associates

Gerald Moorhead

St. Cecilia Catholic Church
Houston TX
11730 Denise
1978
Charles Tapley Associates

Richard Payne

Municipal Control Facility
Missouri City TX
End of Blue Lake Drive
1979
Taft Architects

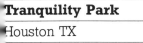

Univ. of Texas at San Antonio
San Antonio TX

1976
Ford Powell & Carson;
Bartlett Cocke & Associates

New Mexico

Albuquerque Museum
Albuquerque NM
2000 Mountain Road N.W.
1979
Antoine Predock

La Luz del Oeste
Residential Community
Albuquerque NM
Coors Rd. nr. Montano Rd. N.W.
1974
Antoine Predock

First Plaza
Albuquerque NM
55 First Plaza
1976
Harry Weese & Associates

Arizona

Scottsdale Center
for the Arts
Scottsdale AZ
7383 Scottsdale Mall
1974
Bennie M. Gonzales, FAIA

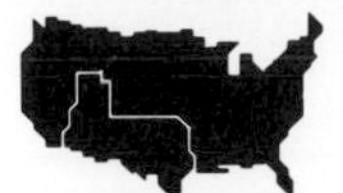

Scottsdale Civic Center
Scottsdale AZ
3939 Civic Center Plaza
1968
Bennie M. Gonzales, FAIA

Neil Koppes

Arcosanti
Scottsdale AZ (Mayer)
Interstate 17 to Cordes Junction
Continuing
Paolo Soleri

Ivan Pintar

Cosanti
Scottsdale AZ
6433 Doubletree Road
Continuing
Paolo Soleri

Ivan Pintar

Taliesin West
Scottsdale AZ
11000 Shea Road
1937–1956
Frank Lloyd Wright

Kitt Peak Observatory
Tucson AZ
Kitt Peak Mountain
1962
Skidmore Owings & Merrill

Ezra Stoller©Esto

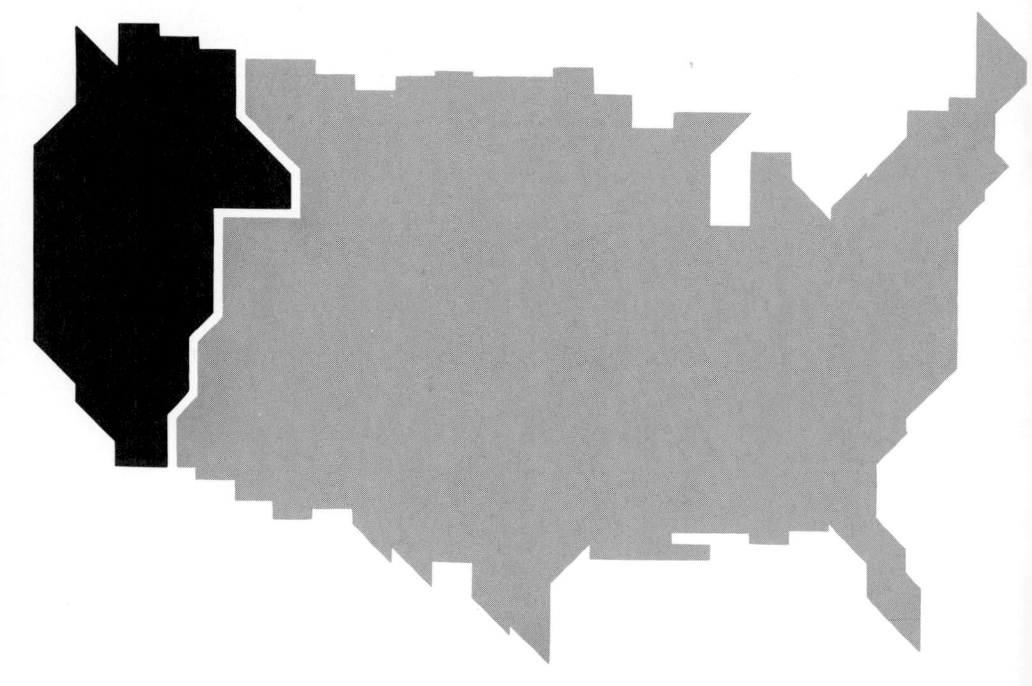

W E S T

Ritter House

Atherton CA (No. Calif.)

349 Selby Lane

1957

Wurster Bernardi & Emmons

UC Student Center Complex

Berkeley CA

University of California Campus

1960–68

DeMars & Reay; Hardison & Komatsu; DeMars & Wells

Wurster Hall

Berkeley CA

University of California Campus

1965

DeMars Esherick & Olson

Weston Havens House

Berkeley CA

255 Panoramic Way

1941

Harwell Hamilton Harris

88″ Cyclotron and Radio-Chemistry Lab

Berkeley CA

UC Berkeley, Cyclotron Road

1960

MBT (McCue Boone Tomsick)

Concord Pavilion
Concord CA (No. Calif.)
2000 Kirker Pass Road
1975
Frank O. Gehry & Associates

© Morley Baer

Garden Grove Community Church
Garden Grove CA (So. Calif.)
12141 Lewis Street
1980
Johnson/Burgee

Gordon Schenck Jr.

Garden Grove Community Church
Garden Grove CA
12141 Lewis Street
1961
Richard J. Neutra

Julius Shulman

Sea Ranch Condominium #1
Gualala, Sonoma County CA
Highway 1, Sea Ranch
1965
MLTW/Moore Lyndon Turnbull Whitaker

© Morley Baer

Fluor Corporation
Irvine CA
3333 Michelson Drive
1981
Welton Becket Associates

Julius Shulman

WILL ROGERS
Riviera
Riviera
Revere
Jr High Sch
MARLBORO
HANOVER
EVANSTON
ROCKINGHAM
Santa Monica
ry Club
SAN VIC
BM
348
LOS ANGELES
SANTA MONICA
BM
324
23D
AVE
21ST
GEORGINA
CARLYLE
20TH
16TH
MARGUERITA
18TH
Fire
Sta
Library
ALTA
Corpus Christi
Sch
303
284
CHAUTAUQUA
Racquet
Country Club
AMALFI
NAPOLI
RIVIERA
292
Santa Monica Canyon
Santa Monica
214
Canyon Sch
LOS ANGELES
SANTA MONICA
BLVD
14TH
ST
SAN VICENTE
SANTA MONICA
1
193
7TH
SAN VICENTE
Roosevelt
Sch
Roosevelt
Sch
12TH
14TH
WASHINGTON
Lincoln
Jr H
10TH
157
W R B S P
BM
162
BM
17
4 LANE
4TH
SANTA MONICA
OCEAN
MONTANA
AVE
PALISADES
6TH
St Monica
High Sch
WILSHIRE
SANT
Madison
Sch
Lincoln
Park
SANTA MONICA BEACH STATE PARK
PARK
AVE
BM 19
103
PO
Library
101
LINCOLN
Fire
Station
1
THE PROMENADE
2D
MALL
4TH
BROADWAY
2
Palisades Park
OCEAN
12
2
Footbridge
4 LANE
City
Hall
BM 64

Brentwood
Brentwood Sch
Library
GORHAM
GRANVILLE
DARLINGTON
KIOWA
WESTGATE
BARRINGTON
GRETNA GREEN
BUNDY
BM 325
Hospital
Administration Center
BDY
BUTLER
St Sebastian Sch
University High Sch
Brockton Ave Sch
Res
Reservoirs
WELLESLEY
BOUNDARY
STANFORD
HARVARD
26TH
Douglas Park
TEXAS
BM 209
BM 241
PO
CH
Sterry Sch
West Los Angeles
WESTGATE
BROCKTON
STONER
FEDERAL
Japanese
NEBRASKA
Stoner Recreation Center
IDAHO
CENTINELA
MISSISSIPPI
OLYMPIC
Santa Monica Jr Academy
SANTA MONICA
Drive-in Theater
BM 153
McKinley Sch
BROADWAY
CLOVERFIELD
4 LANE
EXPOSITION
VIRGINIA
8 LANE
Park
St Anne Sch
ICA
Garfield Sch
10
165
173
Edison Sch
KANSAS
BOUNDARY
28TH
30TH
PEARL
33D
25TH
Grant Sch
23D
21ST
Memorial Park
6 LANE
DELAWARE
Woodlawn Cem
Santa Monica City College
EUCLID
PICO
GRANT
14TH
11TH
Library
OCEAN
PARK
MUNICIPAL AIRPORT
(CLOVER FIELD)
John Adams Jr High Sch
Will Rogers Sch
18TH
BM 134
Radio Facility
DEWEY
ROSE
BM 162
ARMACOST
FREEW
132
175
259
266
376
382

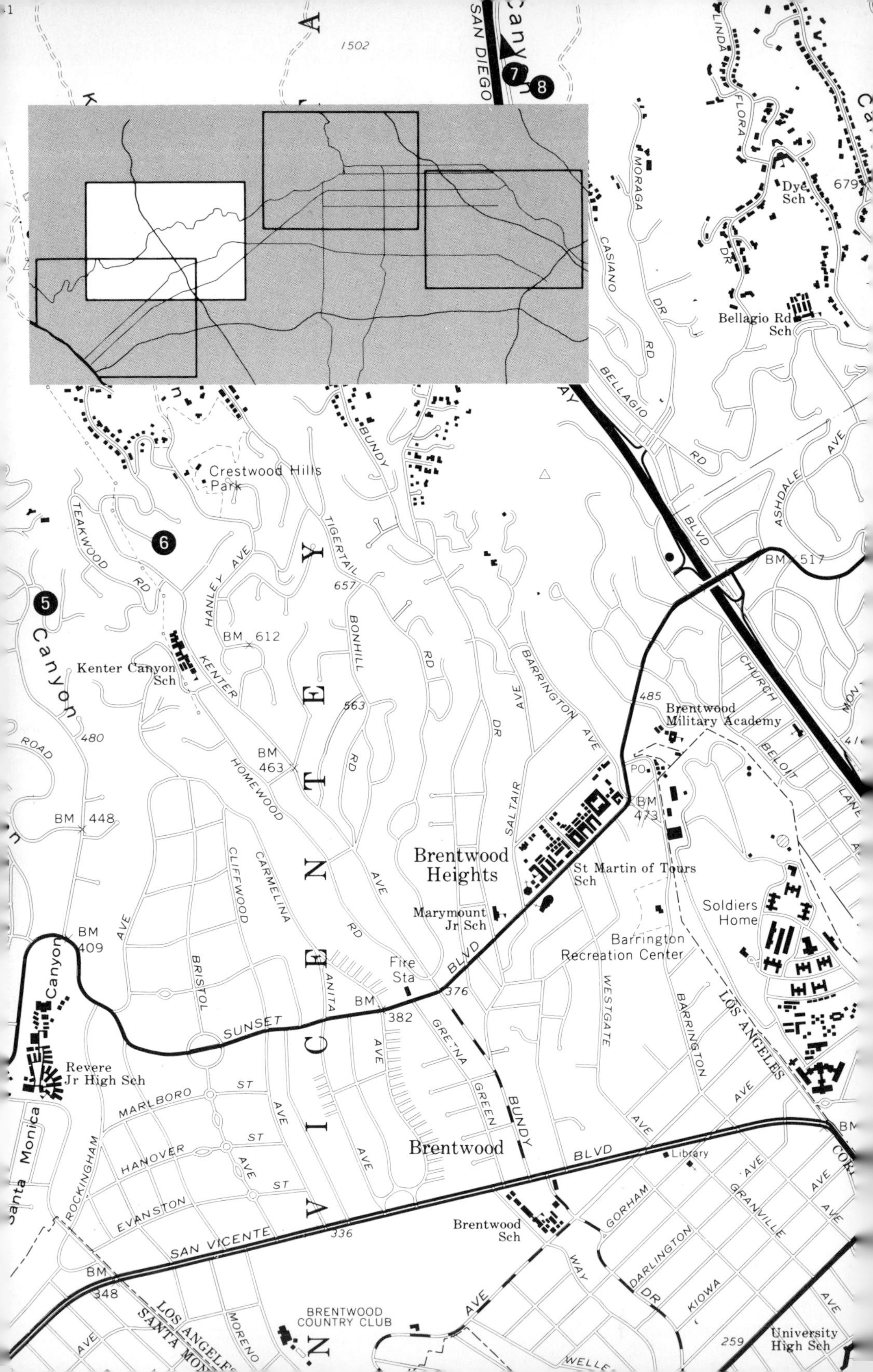

SAN DIEGO
Canyon
1502
FLORA
LINDA
MORAGA
Dye Sch
679
CASIANO
DR
RD
Bellagio Rd Sch
BELLAGIO
RD
BLVD
ASHDALE AVE
BM 517
BUNDY
Crestwood Hills Park
TEAKWOOD
RD
HANLEY AVE
TIGERTAIL
657
BM 612
BONHILL
RD
Canyon
Kenter Canyon Sch
KENTER
563
BARRINGTON
AVE
DR
485
Brentwood Military Academy
CHURCH
BELOIT
ROAD
480
BM 463
HOMEWOOD
RD
SALTAIR
PO
BM 473
LANE
BM 448
CLIFFWOOD
CARMELINA
AVE
Brentwood Heights
St Martin of Tours Sch
Soldiers Home
Marymount Jr Sch
Barrington Recreation Center
AVE
BM 409
Canyon
Fire Sta
BLVD
376
WESTGATE
BARRINGTON
LOS ANGELES
BRISTOL
SUNSET
BM 382
ANITA
AVE
GRETNA
Revere Jr High Sch
MARLBORO
ST
AVE
GREEN
BUNDY
AVE
AVE
Santa Monica
HANOVER
ST
AVE
Brentwood
BLVD
Library
AVE
GRANVILLE
AVE
ROCKINGHAM
EVANSTON
ST
AVE
GORHAM
AVE
SAN VICENTE
336
Brentwood Sch
DARLINGTON
BM 348
WAY
DR
KIOWA
LOS ANGELES
SANTA MONICA
MORENO
BRENTWOOD COUNTRY CLUB
AVE
AVE
259
University High Sch
AVE
SAN VICENTE

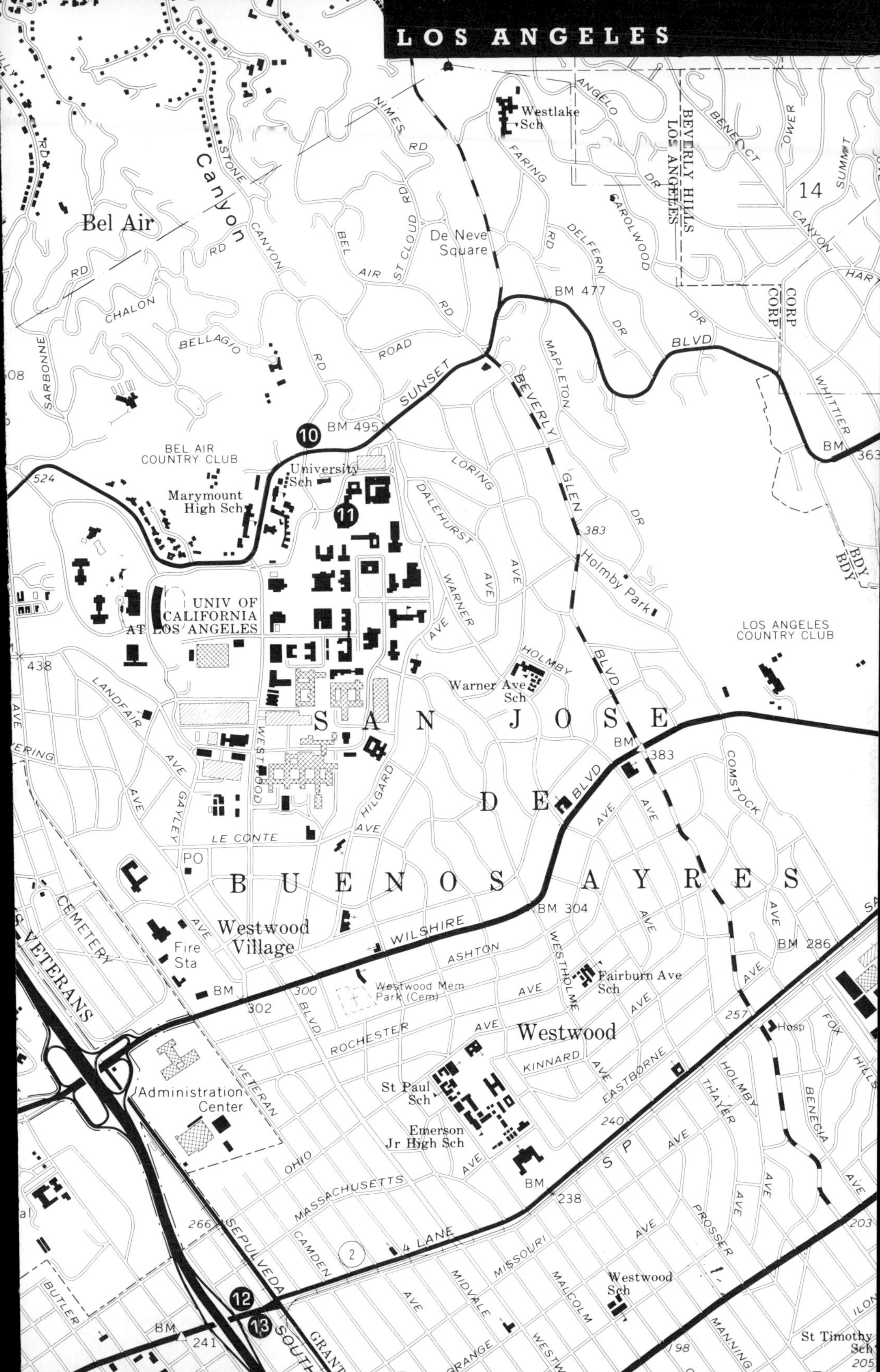
LOS ANGELES
Bel Air
Canyon
Westlake Sch
BEVERLY HILLS
LOS ANGELES
De Neve Square
BM 477
14
CORP
CORP
BM 495
BEL AIR COUNTRY CLUB
University Sch
Marymount High Sch
UNIV OF CALIFORNIA AT LOS ANGELES
Holmby Park
LOS ANGELES COUNTRY CLUB
Warner Ave Sch
SAN JOSE DE BUENOS AYRES
BM 383
PO
Westwood Village
Fire Sta
BM 304
BM 286
Fairburn Ave Sch
Westwood Mem Park (Cem)
BM 302
Westwood
Hosp
Administration Center
St Paul Sch
Emerson Jr High Sch
BM 238
4 LANE
Westwood Sch
BM 241
St Timothy Sch
SUNSET BLVD
BEVERLY GLEN BLVD
WILSHIRE BLVD
SEPULVEDA
VETERANS
CEMETERY
LE CONTE AVE
HILGARD AVE
WESTWOOD BLVD
GAYLEY AVE
LANDFAIR AVE
ASHTON
ROCHESTER AVE
KINNARD AVE
EASTBORNE AVE
OHIO AVE
MASSACHUSETTS
MISSOURI AVE
MIDVALE AVE
MALCOLM
PROSSER
THAYER AVE
HOLMBY AVE
BENECIA AVE
COMSTOCK AVE
WESTHOLME
LORING
DALEHURST AVE
WARNER AVE
MAPLETON DR
DELFERN DR
CAROLWOOD DR
FARING RD
ANGELO
BENEDICT
SUMMIT
CANYON
WHITTIER DR
STONE CANYON RD
CHALON RD
BELLAGIO ROAD
SARBONNE
NIMES RD
ST CLOUD RD
BEL AIR RD
CAMDEN
BUTLER
LAGRANGE
MANNING
GRANT
SP

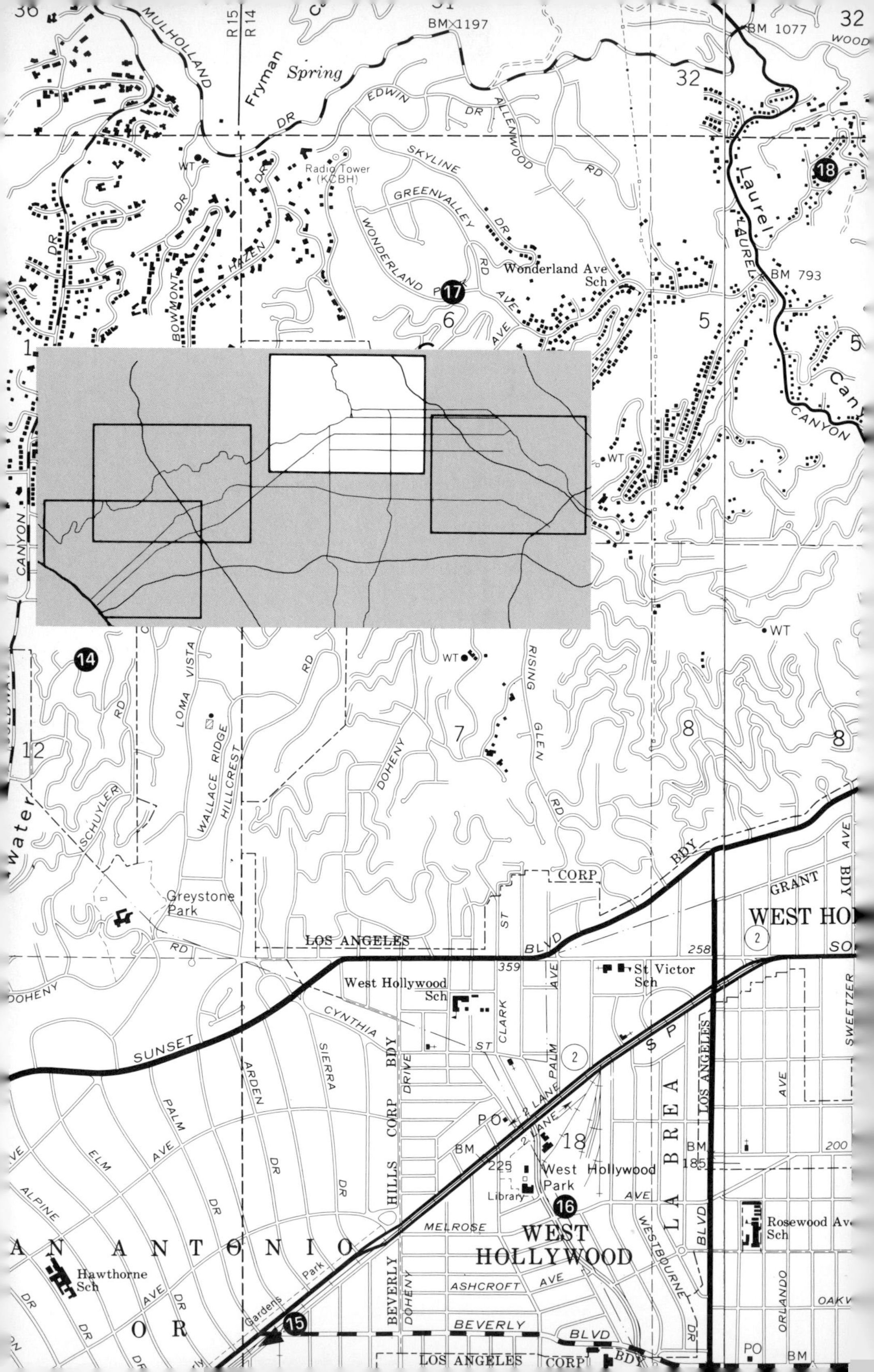

MULHOLLAND
Fryman
Spring
BM 1197
BM 1077
EDWIN
DR
ALLENWOOD
RD
SKYLINE
Radio Tower
(KCBH)
GREENVALLEY
DR
WONDERLAND
RD
AVE
Wonderland Ave
Sch
17
18
Laurel
LAUREL
BM 793
CANYON
HAZEN
BOWMONT
DR
WT
14
LOMA VISTA
WALLACE RIDGE
HILLCREST
SCHUYLER
RD
Greystone
Park
DOHENY
RISING
GLEN
RD
CORP
LOS ANGELES
BDY
GRANT
WEST HO
BLVD
SUNSET
West Hollywood
Sch
St Victor
Sch
CYNTHIA
ST
CLARK
PALM
SIERRA
ARDEN
ELM
AVE
ALPINE
DRIVE
HILLS CORP
BDY
PO
BM
225
West Hollywood
Park
Library
16
MELROSE
WEST
HOLLYWOOD
LA BREA
LOS ANGELES
WESTBOURNE
Rosewood Ave
Sch
SWEETZER
ORLANDO
AN ANTONIO
Hawthorne
Sch
Gardens
Park
15
BEVERLY
BLVD
ASHCROFT
OAKW
LOS ANGELES
CORP
SOL

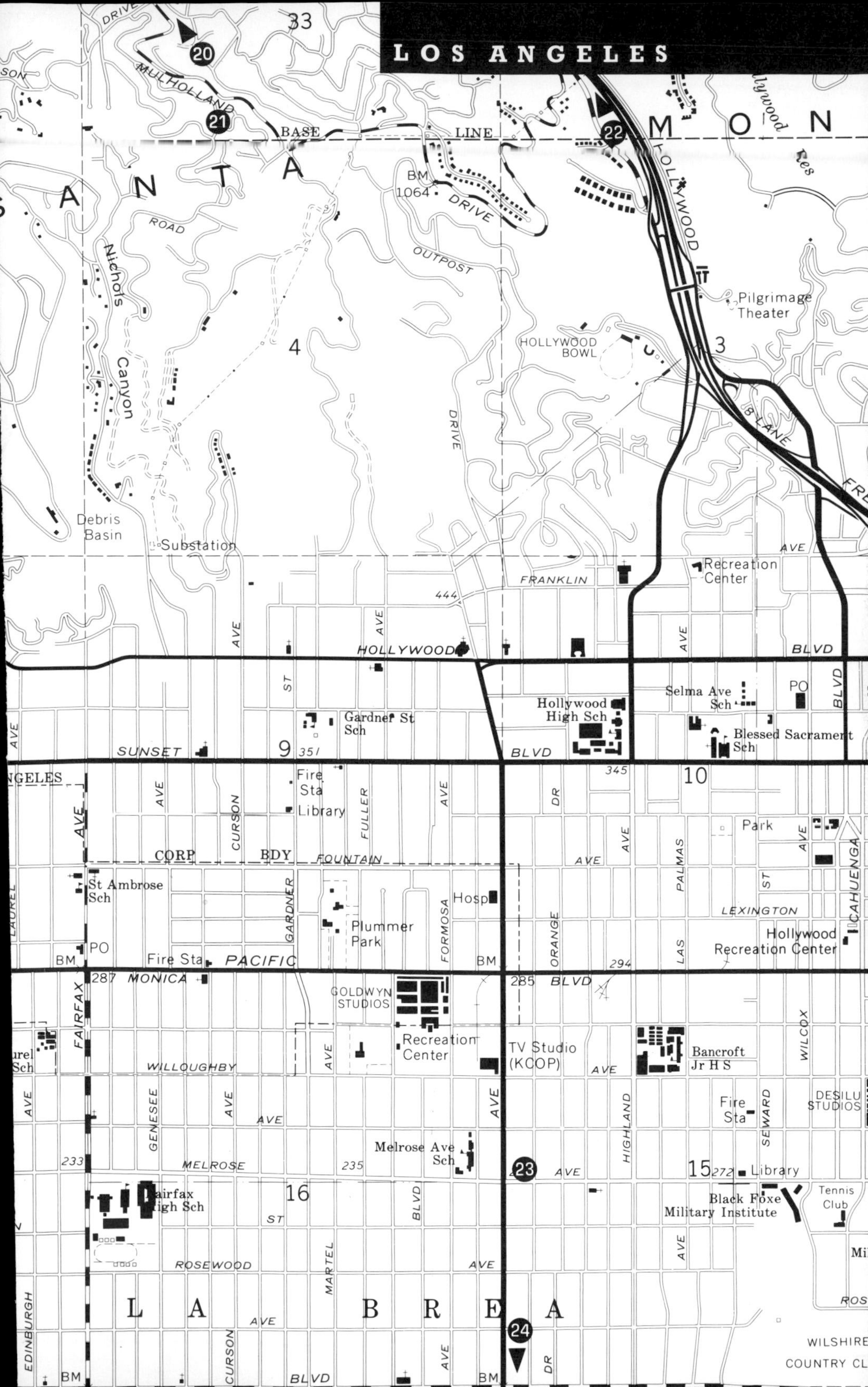
LOS ANGELES
SANTA MONICA
MULHOLLAND
BASE LINE
HOLLYWOOD FREEWAY
Nichols Canyon
Debris Basin
Substation
OUTPOST DRIVE
HOLLYWOOD BOWL
Pilgrimage Theater
FRANKLIN AVE
Recreation Center
HOLLYWOOD BLVD
Selma Ave Sch
Hollywood High Sch
Gardner St Sch
Blessed Sacrament Sch
SUNSET BLVD
Fire Sta
Library
CORP BDY
FOUNTAIN AVE
St Ambrose Sch
Hosp
Plummer Park
LEXINGTON
Hollywood Recreation Center
SANTA MONICA BLVD
GOLDWYN STUDIOS
Recreation Center
TV Studio (KCOP)
Bancroft Jr H S
WILLOUGHBY AVE
DESILU STUDIOS
MELROSE AVE
Melrose Ave Sch
Library
Fairfax High Sch
Black Foxe Military Institute
Tennis Club
ROSEWOOD AVE
LA BREA
WILSHIRE COUNTRY CLUB
FAIRFAX AVE
GARDNER
FORMOSA
ORANGE DR
HIGHLAND AVE
LAS PALMAS
WILCOX
SEWARD
CAHUENGA
CURSON
GENESEE
MARTEL
EDINBURGH
LAUREL
FULLER

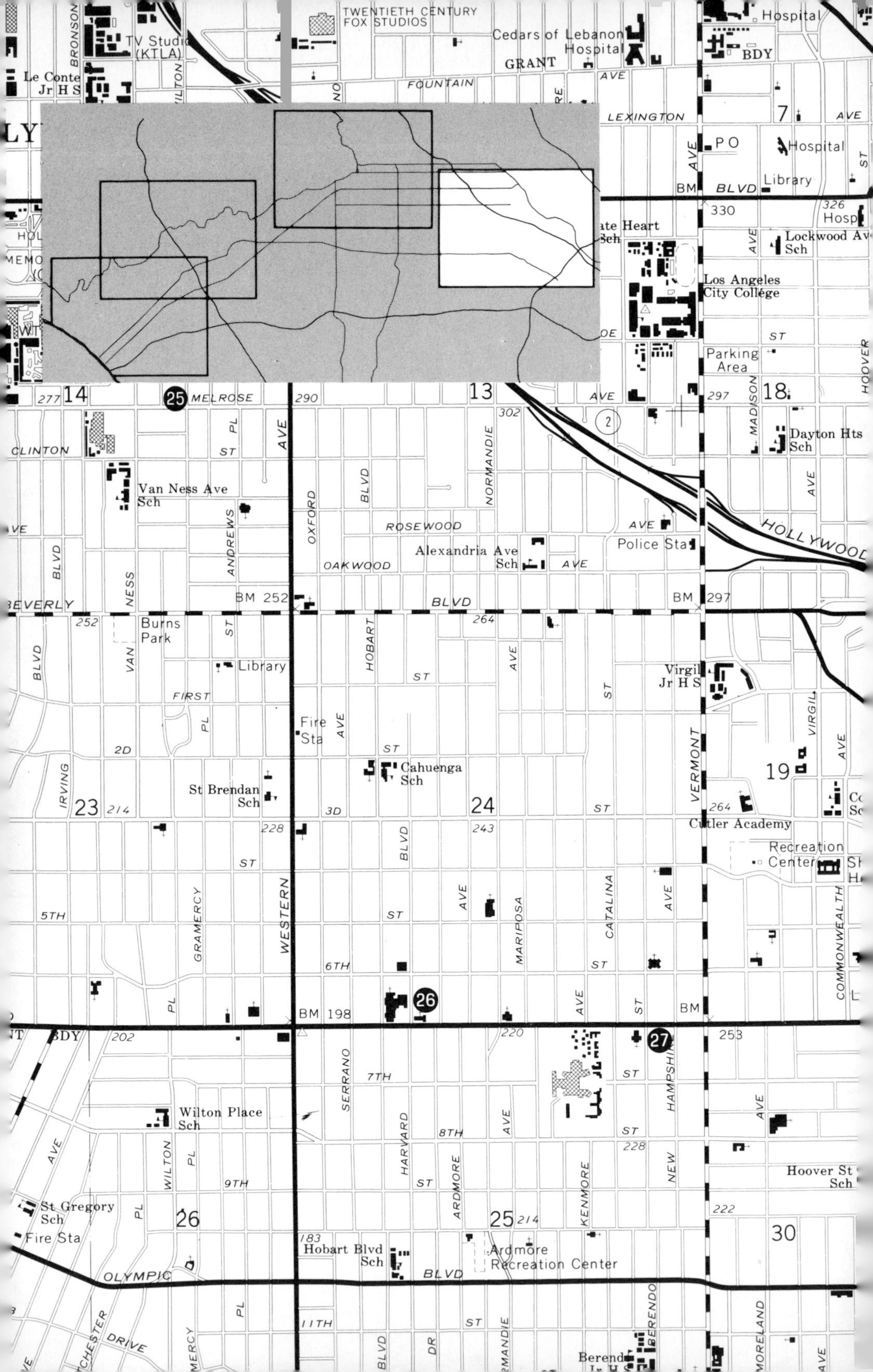

TWENTIETH CENTURY FOX STUDIOS
Cedars of Lebanon Hospital
TV Studio (KTLA)
Le Conte Jr H S
Hospital
Los Angeles City College
Parking Area
Dayton Hts Sch
Van Ness Ave Sch
Alexandria Ave Sch
Police Sta
Burns Park
Library
Virgil Jr H S
Fire Sta
Cahuenga Sch
St Brendan Sch
Cutler Academy
Recreation Center
Wilton Place Sch
Hoover St Sch
St Gregory Sch
Fire Sta
Hobart Blvd Sch
Ardmore Recreation Center
MELROSE AVE
BEVERLY BLVD
HOLLYWOOD
VERMONT AVE
WESTERN AVE
OLYMPIC BLVD

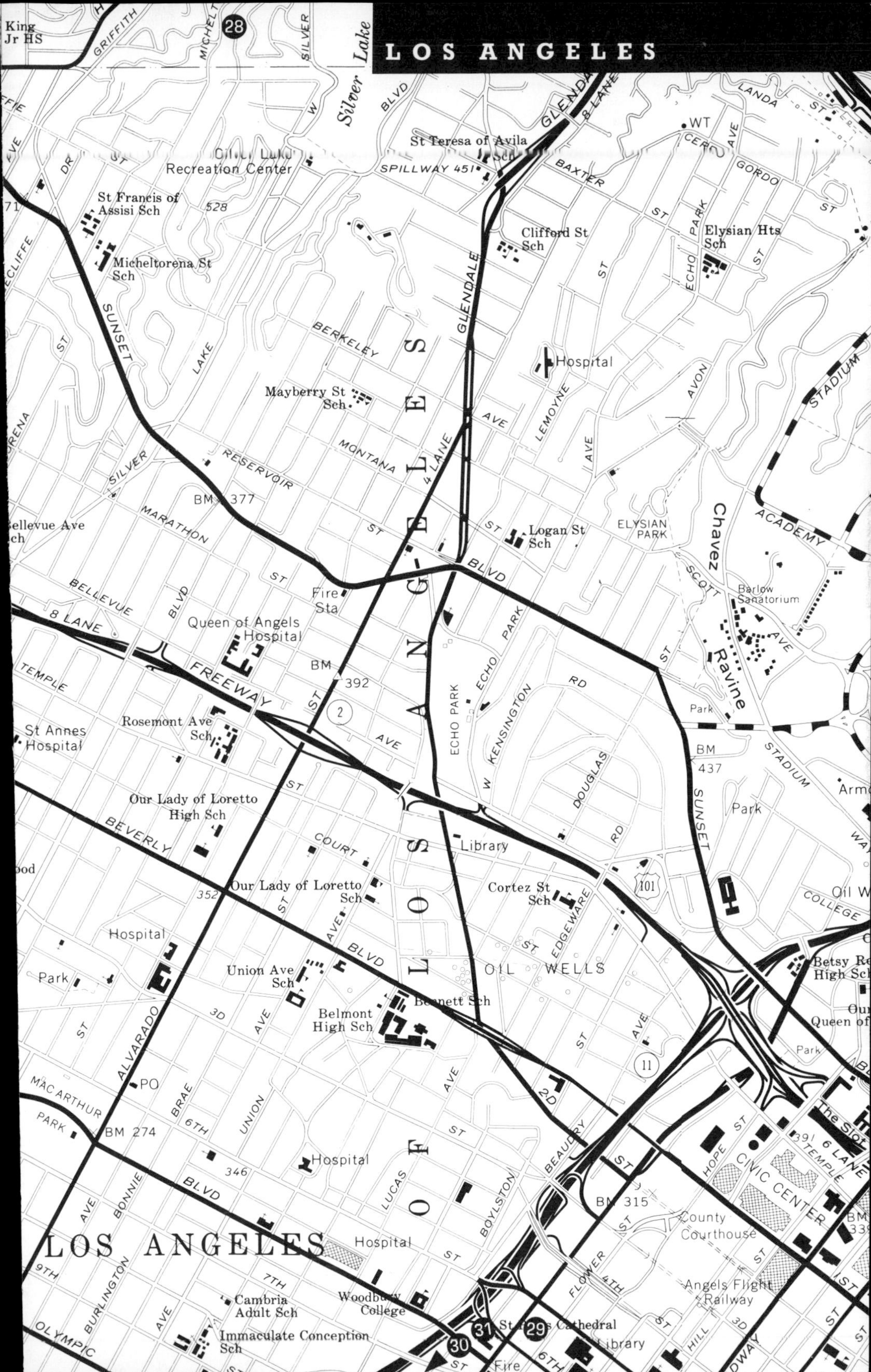
LOS ANGELES
King Jr HS
GRIFFITH
MICHELTORENA
SILVER
Silver Lake
Silver Lake Recreation Center
St Teresa of Avila Sch
SPILLWAY 451
GLENDALE
8 LANE
BAXTER
WT
CERRO GORDO
LANDA
St Francis of Assisi Sch
528
Micheltorena St Sch
Clifford St Sch
Elysian Hts Sch
ECHO PARK
SUNSET
LAKE
BERKELEY
Hospital
LEMOYNE
AVON
STADIUM
Mayberry St Sch
MONTANA
RESERVOIR
SILVER
4 LANE
BM 377
MARATHON
Bellevue Ave Sch
Logan St Sch
ELYSIAN PARK
Chavez Ravine
ACADEMY
BLVD
SCOTT
Barlow Sanatorium
Fire Sta
BELLEVUE
8 LANE
Queen of Angels Hospital
TEMPLE
FREEWAY
BM 392
2
ECHO PARK
KENSINGTON
DOUGLAS
Park
BM 437
St Annes Hospital
Rosemont Ave Sch
Our Lady of Loretto High Sch
BEVERLY
COURT
Library
101
Our Lady of Loretto Sch
352
Cortez St Sch
EDGEWARE
COLLEGE
Hospital
Park
Union Ave Sch
OIL WELLS
Betsy Ross High Sch
Queen of
Belmont High Sch
Bennett Sch
ALVARADO
3D
11
PO
MAC ARTHUR PARK
BM 274
BRAE
6TH
UNION
2D
BEAUDRY
HOPE
The Slot
6 LANE
TEMPLE
CIVIC CENTER
Hospital
346
LUCAS
BOYLSTON
BM 315
County Courthouse
BONNIE
LOS ANGELES
Hospital
9TH
BURLINGTON
7TH
FLOWER
4TH
Angels Flight Railway
Cambria Adult Sch
Woodbury College
OLYMPIC
Immaculate Conception Sch
30
31
St Paul's Cathedral
29
Library
Fire
HILL
3D
1ST
BM 335

Salk Institute for Biological Studies

La Jolla CA (San Diego area)

10010 North Torrey Pines Road

1965

Louis I. Kahn

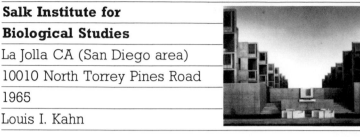

Triad Case Study Houses

La Jolla CA

Rue de Anne

1960

Killingsworth Brady & Smith

Foothill College

Los Altos CA (No. Calif.)

12345 South El Monte Avenue

1961

Ernest J. Kump; Masten & Hurd

Baldwin Hills Village

Los Angeles CA 24

5300 Rodeo Road

1941

Alexander Wilson

Merrill & Johnson

De Bretteville/Simon House

Los Angeles CA 18

8067 & 8071 Willow Glen Road

1976

Peter de Bretteville

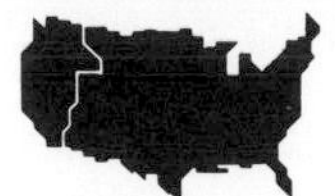

Federal Aviation Agency Building 13

Hawthorne CA

15000 Aviation Boulevard

1973

DMJM

Wayne Thom

One Park Plaza 27

Los Angeles CA

3250 Wilshire Boulevard

1972

DMJM

Wayne Thom

Teledyne Systems Offices & Laboratory 8

Northridge CA

19601 Nordhoff

1967

DMJM

Robert Cleveland

Eames House 1

os Angeles CA

03 Chatauqua Blvd.

949

Charles Eames

Rosen House 5

os Angeles CA

10 Oakmont Drive

962

raig Ellwood Associates

©Morley Baer

Xerox Data Systems (SDS)
El Segundo CA 12
555 South Aviation Blvd.
1966
Craig Ellwood Associates

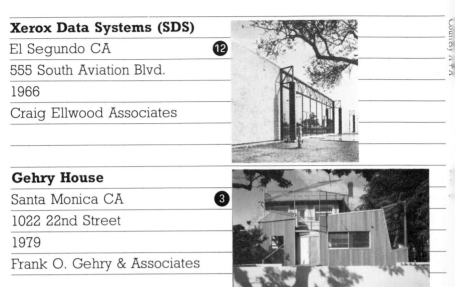

Gehry House
Santa Monica CA 3
1022 22nd Street
1979
Frank O. Gehry & Associates

Danziger Studio-Residence
Los Angeles CA 23
7001 Melrose Avenue
1965
Frank O. Gehry & Associates

Santa Monica Place
Santa Monica CA 2
Broadway and 4th Street
1980
Frank O. Gehry & Associates;
Gruen Associates

Pacific Design Center
Los Angeles CA 16
8687 Melrose Avenue
1976
Gruen Associates

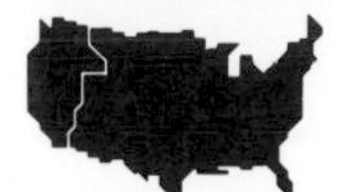

Los Angeles County Health Center 25

Los Angeles CA

5205 Melrose Avenue

1968

Honnold & Rex

Richard Koch

University Research Library

Los Angeles CA 11

UCLA

1964

A. Quincy Jones & Frederick E. Emmons

Julius Shulman

Mutual Housing (100 Houses)

Los Angeles CA 6

1000 Kenter Avenue to end

1950

A. Quincy Jones; Whitney Smith; Edgardo Contini

Emiel Becsky

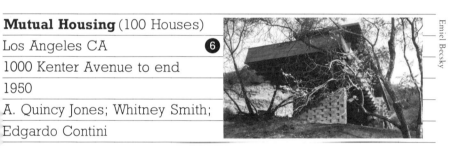

Arts & Architecture Case Study House 21 

Los Angeles CA

9036 Wonderland Park Avenue

1959

Pierre Koenig

Julius Shulman

Silvertop

Los Angeles CA 

2138 Micheltorena Street

1963

John Lautner

Malin (Chemosphere) House

Los Angeles CA 20

7776 Torreyson Drive

1960

John Lautner

St. Basil Catholic Church

Los Angeles CA 26

3611 Wilshire Boulevard

1969

Albert C. Martin & Associates

Julius Shulman

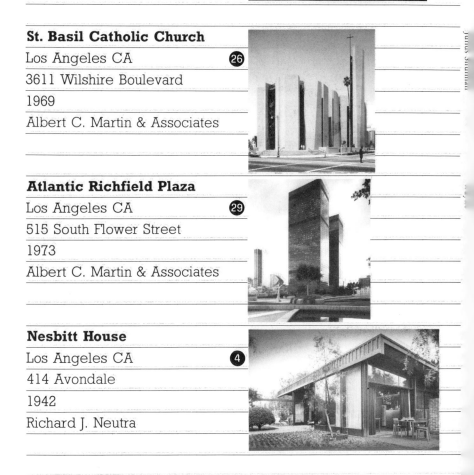

Atlantic Richfield Plaza

Los Angeles CA 

515 South Flower Street

1973

Albert C. Martin & Associates

Nesbitt House

Los Angeles CA 

414 Avondale

1942

Richard J. Neutra

Watts Towers

Los Angeles CA 

1727 East 107th Street

1951

Simon Rodia

Bethlehem Baptist Church
Los Angeles CA 30
4900 Compton Avenue
1944
R. M. Schindler

Esther McCoy

Tischler House
Los Angeles CA 9
175 Greenfield Avenue
1949
R. M. Schindler

Esther McCoy

Dekker House
Canoga Park CA 7
230 Renfield Avenue
940
. M. Schindler

Esther McCoy

chulitz House
everly Hills CA 14
356 Lloydcrest Drive
976
elmut D. Schulitz;
ban Innovations Group

olby Apartments
s Angeles CA 15
everly Green Dr. & Vidor St.
50
phael Soriano

Curtis House

Los Angeles CA 10

111 Stone Canyon Road

1950

Raphael Soriano

Shulman House

Los Angeles CA 19

7875 Woodrow Wilson Drive

1950

Raphael Soriano

Adolph Building

Burbank CA 22

1800 West Magnolia Blvd.

1953

Raphael Soriano

General Panel House

Los Angeles CA 21

2861 Nichols Canyon Road

1950

Konrad Wachsmann &

Walter Gropius

Los Gatos Civic Center

Los Gatos CA (No. Calif.)

100 East Main Street

1967

Stickney & Hull, AIA

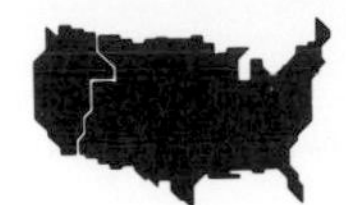

Davis House

Malibu CA (Los Angeles Area)

29715 Cuthbert Avenue

1972

Frank O. Gehry & Associates

Tim Street-Porter

Two Houses

Mill Valley CA (No. Calif.)

20 & 24 Longfellow Road

1952

Raphael Soriano

Chapel, Mills College

Oakland CA

Mills College Campus

1967

Callister Payne & Bischoff

Philip Molten

Clorox Building

Oakland CA

1221 Broadway

1975

Gruen Associates

Jeremiah Bragstad

Wells Fargo Bank Building

Oakland CA

1333 Broadway

1973

Gruen Associates

Balthazar Korab

The Oakland Museum

Oakland CA

1000 Oak Street

1968

Kevin Roche John Dinkeloo & Associates

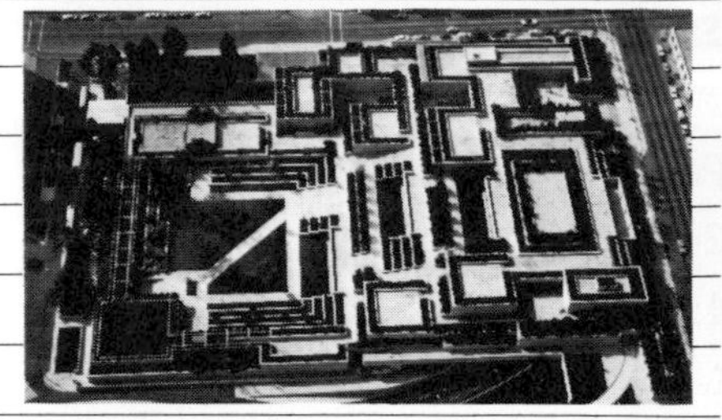

Wyle House

Ojai CA (Santa Barbara Area)

1964 Rancho Drive

1948

Harwell Hamilton Harris

Moore House

Ojai CA

512 North Foothill

1953

Richard J. Neutra

Elrod House

Palm Springs CA

2175 Southridge Drive

1968

John Lautner

Toole House

Palm Village (Indian Wells) CA

75297 Highway 111

1947

R. M. Schindler

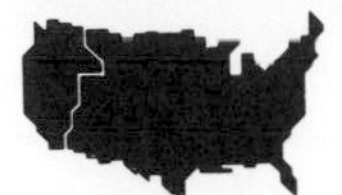

Syntex Research & Administration Center
Palo Alto CA
3401 Hillview Avenue
1972
MBT (McCue Boone Tomsick)

Jeremiah Bragstad

Stanford Employees Credit Union
Palo Alto CA
Stanford University
1964
Ezra Ehrenkrantz; Robertson Ward

Center for Advanced Study in Behavioral Sciences
Palo Alto CA
Stanford University
1955
Wurster Bernardi & Emmons

© Morley Baer

Wayfarers Chapel
Palos Verdes CA
5755 Palos Verdes Drive South
1949
Lloyd Wright

Julius Shulman

Art Center College of Design
Pasadena CA (Los Angeles Area)
1700 Lida Street
1976
Craig Ellwood Associates

Marvin Rand

Chevron Research Lab "D"
Richmond CA (No. Calif.)
576 Standard Avenue
1967
MBT (McCue Boone Tomsick)

© Morley Baer

Notch Project
Sacramento CA
1901 Arden Way
1977
SITE

San Bernardino City Hall
San Bernardino CA (So. Calif.)
300 North D Street
1972
Gruen Associates

Security Pacific Bank
San Bernardino CA
Fourth and D Streets
1972
Gruen Associates

San Diego Stadium
San Diego CA
Mission Valley
1967
Hope Consulting Group

ZLAC Rowing Club
Boathouse Addition
San Diego CA
1111 Pacific Beach Drive
1963
Sim Bruce Richards

Aquatic Control Center
San Diego CA
2581 Quivira Court
1961
Sim Bruce Richards

The Cannery ❶
San Francisco CA
500 Beach Street
1968
Esherick Homsey Dodge

Kathleen Kershaw

St. Francis Square
Cooperative Apartments ❷
San Francisco CA
10 Bertie Lane
1963
Marquis & Stoller

Karl Rick

Commodore Sloat
Elementary School ❸
San Francisco CA
50 Darien Way
1977
Marquis Associates

Rondal Partridge

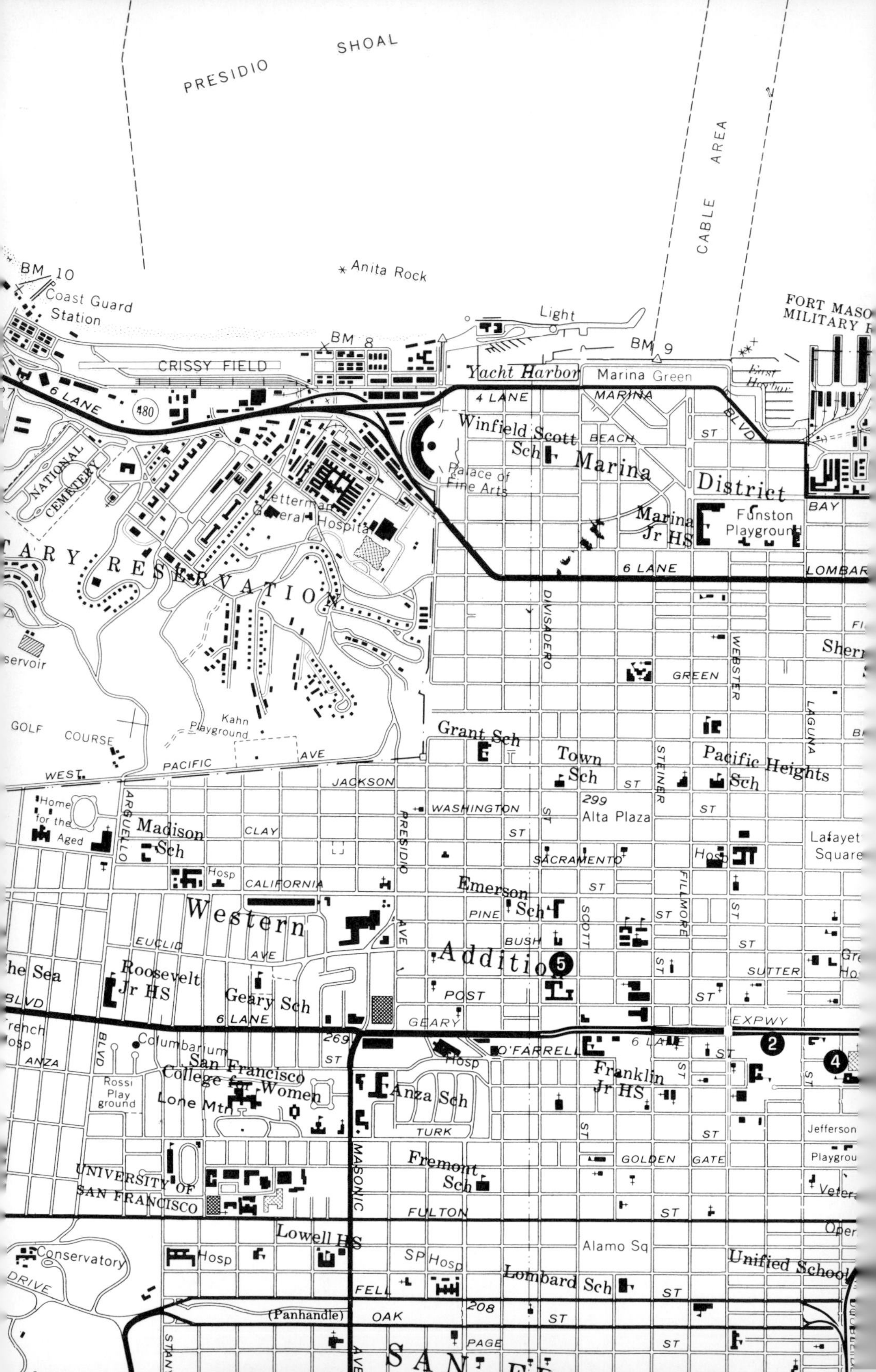
PRESIDIO SHOAL
CABLE AREA
Anita Rock
BM 10
Coast Guard Station
BM 8
Light
BM 9
FORT MASON MILITARY
CRISSY FIELD
Yacht Harbor
Marina Green
East Harbor
6 LANE
480
4 LANE
MARINA BLVD
Winfield Scott Sch
BEACH
ST
Marina District
NATIONAL CEMETERY
Palace of Fine Arts
Letterman General Hospital
Marina Jr HS
Funston Playground
BAY
MILITARY RESERVATION
6 LANE
LOMBARD
DIVISADERO
Reservoir
WEBSTER
GREEN
LAGUNA
GOLF COURSE
Kahn Playground
Grant Sch
Town Sch
STEINER
Pacific Heights Sch
WEST PACIFIC AVE
JACKSON
ST
ST
Home for the Aged
ARGUELLO
Madison Sch
CLAY
WASHINGTON
PRESIDIO
299
Alta Plaza
ST
Lafayette Square
SACRAMENTO
Hosp
Hosp
CALIFORNIA
Emerson Sch
ST
FILLMORE
Western Addition
PINE
SCOTT
ST
ST
EUCLID
AVE
BUSH
ST
ST
5
SUTTER
Roosevelt Jr HS
Geary Sch
POST
ST
BLVD
6 LANE
GEARY
EXPWY
French Hosp
ANZA
BLVD
Columbarium
269
ST
O'FARRELL
6 LANE
ST
2
4
San Francisco College for Women
Hosp
Franklin Jr HS
Rossi Play ground
Lone Mtn
Anza Sch
TURK
ST
Jefferson Playground
MASONIC
Fremont Sch
GOLDEN GATE
UNIVERSITY OF SAN FRANCISCO
FULTON
ST
Opera
Lowell HS
Alamo Sq
Conservatory
Hosp
SP Hosp
Unified School
DRIVE
Lombard Sch
FELL
ST
(Panhandle)
OAK
208
ST
PAGE
ST
AVE
SAN

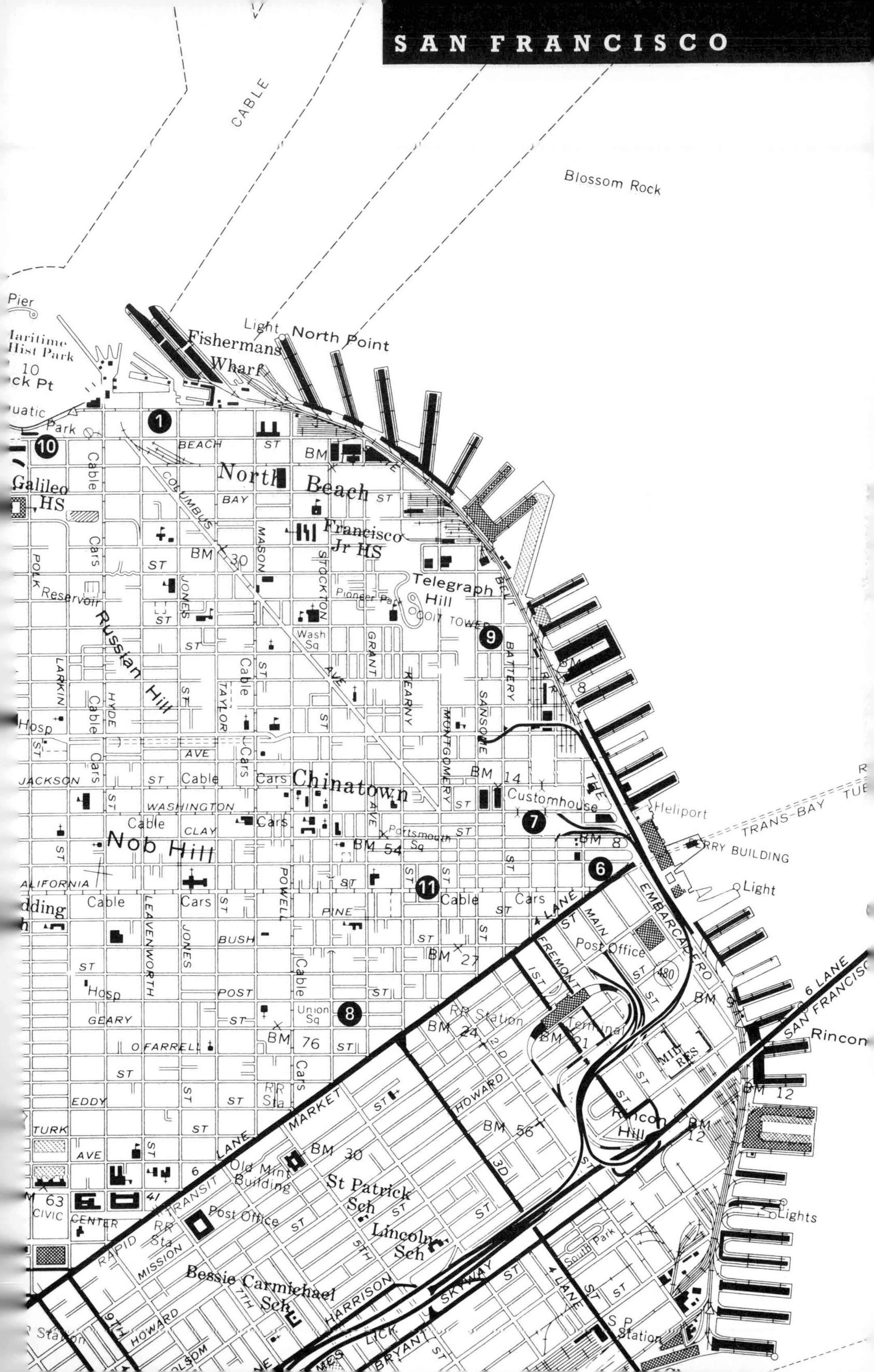
CABLE
Blossom Rock
Pier
Maritime Hist Park
Aquatic Park
Light
North Point
Fishermans Wharf
1
10
BEACH ST
North Beach
BAY
COLUMBUS
Galileo HS
Cable Cars
Francisco Jr HS
BM 30
MASON
STOCKTON
POLK
Reservoir
Russian Hill
JONES
Telegraph Hill
Pioneer Park
COIT TOWER
9
BELT
Wash Sq
GRANT
KEARNY
BATTERY
SANSOME
LARKIN
HYDE
TAYLOR
AVE
MONTGOMERY
JACKSON
Chinatown
Customhouse
7
Heliport
TRANS-BAY
FERRY BUILDING
WASHINGTON
CLAY
Portsmouth Sq
BM 54
BM 14
BM 8
6
Nob Hill
CALIFORNIA
POWELL
11
Light
EMBARCADERO
LEAVENWORTH
PINE
BUSH
4 LANE
FREMONT
MAIN
Post Office
480
BM 27
POST
Union Sq
8
GEARY
O FARRELL
BM 76
RR Station
Terminal
BM 24
BM 21
6 LANE
SAN FRANCISCO
Rincon
BM 12
MIL RES
EDDY
TURK
MARKET
HOWARD
BM 56
Rincon Hill
6 LANE
RR Sta
Old Mint Building
BM 30
3D
2D
1ST
St Patrick Sch
CIVIC CENTER
RAPID TRANSIT
Post Office
MISSION
5TH
Lincoln Sch
South Park
Lights
Bessie Carmichael Sch
7TH
HARRISON
SKYWAY
4 LANE
9TH
HOWARD
FOLSOM
BRYANT
S P Station

St. Mary's Cathedral

San Francisco CA 4

Gouch Street near Geary Street

1971

McSweeney Ryan & Lee;

Pietro Belluschi/Pier Luigi Nervi

©Morley Baer

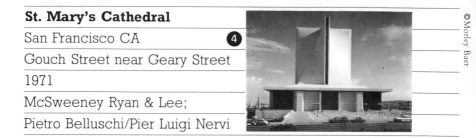

Maimonides (Mount Zion) **Hospital** 5

San Francisco CA

2356 Sutter Street

1950

Eric Mendelsohn

Esther McCoy

Hyatt Regency Hotel

San Francisco CA 

5 Embarcadero Center

1974

John Portman & Associates

Alcoa Building

San Francisco CA 7

One Maritime Plaza

1967

Skidmore Owings & Merrill

Morris Store, Maiden Lane

San Francisco CA 8

140 Maiden Lane

1949

Frank Lloyd Wright

The Ice House

San Francisco CA 9

151 Union Street

1968

Wurster Bernardi & Emmons

© Morley Baer

Ghirardelli Square

San Francisco CA 10

900 North Point Street

1969

Wurster Bernardi & Emmons;

Lawrence Halprin & Associates

Ernest Braun

Bank of America World HQ

San Francisco CA 11

555 California Street

1971

Wurster Bernardi & Emmons;

SOM; Pietro Belluschi

Ezra Stoller ©Esto

IBM Santa Teresa Laboratory

San Jose CA

555 Bailey Avenue

1978

MBT (McCue Boone Tomsick)

Marvin Wax

Marin County Civic Center

San Rafael CA (No. Calif.)

No. San Pedro Rd. & U.S. 101

1957–1972

Frank Lloyd Wright;

Taliesen Associates

Esther McCoy

Hearst Castle
San Simeon CA
State Highway 1
1947
Julia Morgan

Esther McCoy

World Savings & Loan
Santa Ana CA (So. Calif.)
3820 S. Bristol
1978
Kamnitzer Cotton Vreeland

Tim Street-Porter

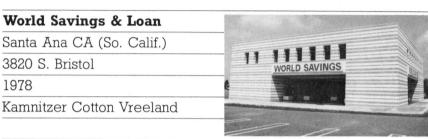

Clark Kerr Learning Center
Santa Barbara CA
Univ. of Calif. Santa Barbara
1972
Marquis & Stoller

Ezra Stoller©Esto

Faculty Club
Santa Barbara CA
Univ. of Calif. Santa Barbara
1968
MLTW/Moore Turnbull

Warren Tremaine House
Santa Barbara CA (Montecito)
1636 Moore Road
1948
Richard J. Neutra

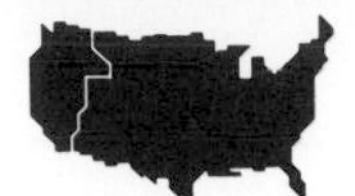

Vedanta Temple

Santa Barbara CA (Montecito)

901 Ladera Lane

1955

Lutah M. Riggs

Esther McCoy

Oakes College

Santa Cruz CA (No. Calif.)

Univ. of Calif. Santa Cruz

1976

MBT (McCue Boone Tomsick)

Jeremiah Bragstad

Kresge College

Santa Cruz CA

Univ. of Calif. Santa Cruz

1973

MLTW/Moore Turnbull

© Morley Baer

Performing Arts Center

Santa Cruz CA

Univ. of Calif. Santa Cruz

1968

Ralph Rapson & Associates

Schuckl & Co.

(Calif. Canners & Growers)

Sunnyvale CA

82 South Fairoaks Avenue

1942

William Wilson Wurster

Roger Sturtevant

Cabrillo Marine Museum

Wilmington CA (LA Area)

3720 Stephen White Drive

1981

Frank O. Gehry & Associates

Oregon

Mt. Angel Benedictine Abbey Library

Mount Angel OR

Salem to Woodbury to Mt. Angel

1970

Alvar Aalto

Equitable Savings & Loan

Portland OR

4215 S.W. 6th Avenue

1948

Pietro Belluschi

Portland Public Office Bldg.

Portland OR

5th St. between Main & Madison

1981

Michael Graves

Auditorium Forecourt Fountain

Portland OR

3rd St. between Market & Clay

1970

Lawrence Halprin & Associates

Lovojoy Plaza & Fountain
Portland OR
Pedestrian Mall
1967
Lawrence Halprin & Associates

John Donat

Martin Stadium
Replacement Seating
Pullman WA
Washington State University
1975
The NBBJ Group

Wayne Thom

Federal Office Building
Seattle WA
915 Second Avenue
1974
John Graham & Co.; Fred Bassetti

Space Needle
Seattle WA
Seattle Center
1962
John Graham & Company

Dudley, Hardin & Young

Winkenwerder Forest
Sciences Laboratory
Seattle WA
University of Washington
1963
Grant Copeland & Chervenak

Hugh Stradford

Condon Hall
Seattle WA
University of Washington
1975
Mitchell/Giurgola

Childrens Orthopedic Hospital & Medical Center
Seattle WA
4800 Sand Point Way
1977
The NBBJ Group

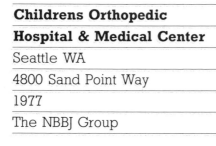

Weyerhaeuser Headquarters Office Building
Tacoma WA
2525 South 336th Street
1972
Skidmore Owings & Merrill

Idaho

Boise Cascade Building
Boise ID
One Jefferson Square
1972
Skidmore Owings & Merrill

Associated Students Activity Center
Moscow ID
University of Idaho
1975
Cline Smull Hamill Quintieri

Utah

Cliff Lodge

Mid Gap UT (Snowbird Ski Resort)

Route from Salt Lake City to Alta

1976

Enteleki

Gordon Peery

Mountain View High School

Orem UT

665 West Center Street

1980

Fowler Ferguson Kingston Ruben

Gordon Peery

Bicentennial Arts Center

Salt Lake City UT

South Temple & West Temple

1980

Fowler Ferguson Kingston Ruben

Earle Eppich

Nevada

Las Vegas Strip & Downtown

Las Vegas NV

1940 to Present

Garish & Greed, Architects

Hawaii

Ke-ahole Airport

Kona HI

1971

Aotani & Oka

Julius Shulman

Garden Office Building

Honolulu HI

1210 Auahi Street

1969

Chapman Cobeen Desai Sakata

Augie Salbosa

Kukui Gardens

Honolulu HI

Vineyard Blvd. & Aala Street

1970

DMJM

DNA

Graduate Research Library

Honolulu HI

Univ. of Hawaii, Manoa Campus

1968

A. Quincy Jones & Frederick
E. Emmons; Hogan & Chapman

Wayne Thom

Kahala Hilton Hotel

Honolulu HI

5000 Kahala Avenue

1963

Killingsworth Brady & Smith

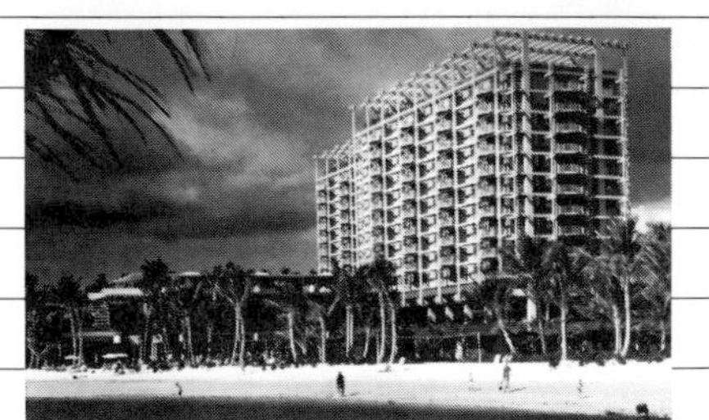

St. Sylvester's Church

Kilauea Kauai HI

Address to come

1958

John H. McAuliffe, Jr.;
Edwin L. Bauer

Honolulu Municipal Building

Honolulu HI

King and Punchbowl Streets

1975

The NBBJ Group

Wayne Thom

John F. Kennedy Theater

Honolulu HI

University of Hawaii

1962

I. M. Pei Associates;

Young & Henderson

James Y. Young

Jefferson Hall

Honolulu HI

University of Hawaii

1962

I. M. Pei Associates;

Young & Henderson

James Y. Young

Mauna Kea Beach Hotel

Kamuela HI

1965

Skidmore Owings & Merrill

Financial Plaza of the Pacific

Honolulu HI

Fort & Merchant Streets

1969

Leo S. Wou; Gruen Associates

Photo Hawaii

B I B L I O G R A P H Y

Alabama

Downtown Birmingham: Architectural and Historical Walking Tour Guide
Marjorie L. White; Richard Sprague; G. Gray Plossner, Jr.

California

A Guide to Architecture in Los Angeles and Southern California
David Gebhard and Robert Winter

The Architecture of Los Angeles
Paul Gleye; Julius Shulman; Bruce Boehne

A Guide to Architecture in San Francisco and Northern California
David Gebhard; Roger Montgomery; Robert Winter

AIA Guide to San Diego
San Diego Chapter AIA

The Sidewalk Companion to Santa Cruz Architecture
John Chase

Colorado

Denver Landmarks
Langdon E. Morris, Jr.

Connecticut

New Haven: A Guide to Architecture and Urban Design
Elizabeth Mills Brown

District of Columbia

A Guide to the Architecture of Washington, D.C.
Warren J. Cox; Hugh Newell Jacobsen; Francis Lethbridge

Walking Tours: Washington, D.C.
Tony P. Wrenn

Illinois

Chicago's Famous Buildings
Ira J. Bach

Indiana

Columbus, Indiana: A Look at Architecture
Columbus Chamber of Commerce

Indianapolis Architecture
Indiana Architectural Foundation

Iowa

The Prairie School in Iowa
Richard G. Wilson and Sidney K. Robinson

Massachusetts	Victorian Boston Today: Ten Walking Tours Pauline Chase Harrell and Margaret Supplee Smith
	Architecture Boston Boston Society of Architects
Michigan	Detroit Architecture Katherine M. Meyer and Martin McElroy
Minnesota	A Guide to the Architecture of Minnesota David Gebhard and Tom Martinson
Missouri	Kansas City Kansas City Chapter AIA
New Hampshire	New Hampshire Architecture: An Illustrated Guide Bryant F. Tolles, Jr. with Carolyn K. Tolles
New Mexico	New Mexico Architecture Bainbridge Bunting and John Conron
New York	New York Landmarks: A Study and Index of Architecturally Notable Structures in Greater New York Alan Burnham
	AIA Guide to New York City Norval White and Elliot Willensley
	The City Observed: New York (A Guide to the Architecture of Manhattan) Paul Goldberger
Texas	Dallasights: An Anthology of Architecture and Open Spaces Dallas Chapter AIA
	San Antonio: A History and Pictorial Guide Charles Ramsdell; Revised by Carmen Perry
Washington	A Guide to Architecture in Washington State Sally Woodbridge and Roger Montgomery

INDEX BY ARCHITECTS

INDEX BY CITIES